Cook
the
Pantry

Also by Robin Robertson

Vegan Without Borders

Vegan Planet

1,000 Vegan Recipes

More Quick-Fix Vegan

Quick-Fix Vegan

Quick-Fix Vegetarian

One-Dish Vegan

Fresh from the Vegan Slow Cooker

Hot Vegan

The Nut Butter Cookbook

Vegan on the Cheap

Party Vegan

The Vegetarian Meat and Potatoes Book

Cook
the
Pantry

Vegan Pantry-to-Plate Recipes in **20 Minutes (or Less!)**

Robin Robertson

VEGAN HERITAGE PRESS

Woodstock • Virginia

Cook the Pantry: Vegan Pantry-to-Plate Recipes in 20 Minutes or Less by Robin Robertson (Copyright © 2015 by Robin Robertson)

ISBN 13: 978-1-941252-18-5

First Edition, October 2015
10 9 8 7 6 5 4 3 2 1

Vegan Heritage Press, LLC books are available at quantity discounts. For information, please visit our website at www. veganheritagepress.com or write the publisher at Vegan Heritage Press, P.O. Box 628, Woodstock, VA 22664-0628.

Library of Congress Cataloging-in-Publication Data
Robertson, Robin (Robin G.)
  Cook the pantry : vegan pantry-to-plate recipes in 20 minutes or less / Robin Robertson. -- First Edition.
    pages cm
  Cook the Pantry is a comprehensive revision of Vegan Unplugged: A Pantry Cuisine Cookbook and Survival Guide by Jon Robertson and Robin Robertson.
  ISBN 978-1-941252-18-5 (paperback) -- ISBN 978-1-941252-19-2 (epub) -- ISBN 978-1-941252-20-8   1.   Vegan cooking. 2. Quick and easy cooking. I. Title.
  TX837.R62376 2015
  641.5′636--dc23
                    2015018488

Cover Design: Annie Oliverio. **Photo Credits:** Cover and recipe photos by Annie Oliverio. **Cover Photo:** Paella from the Pantry (page 92). Incidental photos from stock photo sources include Pantry Bulgur Pilaf (page 104), Chocolate-Almond Truffles (page 145), and chapter opening photo spreads.

Disclaimer: The information provided in this book should not be taken as medical advice. If you require a medical diagnosis or prescription, or if you are contemplating any major dietary change, juice fast, or change in your exercise habits, consult a qualified health-care provider. You should always seek an expert medical opinion before making changes in your diet or supplementation regimen. Neither the publisher nor the author are responsible for readers' health issues.

Publisher's Note: The information in this book is correct and complete to the best of our knowledge. Website addresses and contact information were correct at the time of publication. The publisher is not responsible for specific health or allergy issues or adverse reactions to recipes contained in this book.

Vegan Heritage Press books are distributed by Andrews McMeel Publishing.

Printed in the United States of America

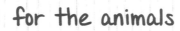

for the animals

Contents

Introduction

Several years ago my husband Jon and I wrote a book based on our experiences of cooking without power in the aftermath of a strong hurricane. The book, *Vegan Unplugged*, was filled with advice for managing life in a home without electricity, along with 70 recipes one can make using only pantry ingredients and a single-burner butane stove.

The positive feedback for *Vegan Unplugged* was tremendous, with people telling us they used the recipes not only for power outages and travel, but also as quick, go-to recipes to make any time (not just when the power was out). We also heard from college students who appreciated the easy 15-minute recipes that didn't require the use of a full kitchen.

But we heard from many others as well—those who loved the recipes but wanted to incorporate fresh ingredients into them in order to make the suitable for everyday cooking. So, in *Cook the Pantry*, the advice on emergency preparedness and cooking without power has been eliminated and fresh ingredients (and lots of new recipes) have been added.

Cook the Pantry is a cookbook that celebrates pantry cooking with recipes that rely mostly on what's on your pantry shelf and in your freezer, but with the inclusion of some fresh ingredients as well. The result is the best of both worlds: the convenience of pantry ingredients and the flavor and nutrition of fresh ingredients. Best of all, all these recipes can be made in 20 minutes or less, for the ultimate in convenience cooking.

As a former restaurant chef and author of over twenty cookbooks, my default setting is to cook from scratch. But on those days when time is short and hunger looms, I also love the convenience of a quick meal using ingredients from my pantry or freezer. Add some fresh produce to the meal, and a good thing becomes even better.

Cook the Pantry empowers you to make the most of your on-hand ingredients by using what's already in your pantry, refrigerator, and freezer to make delicious meals in minutes with a variety of flavorful and nutritious plant-based ingredients.

When you think about it, every good meal begins with a look in the pantry for inspiration. *Cook the Pantry* shows you how to use your pantry to jump-start any meal. Just add fresh produce and proteins to make the more than 100 recipes in this book, many of which can be made with pantry ingredients alone. With *Cook the Pantry*, you can transform your everyday staples into extraordinary meals.

1

Pantry Perfect Cooking

Many of us are often too busy to prepare complicated recipes with long cooking times. Sometimes it's tough enough to find the time or energy to even boil water. That's where *Cook the Pantry* can help. The recipes in this book are made with ingredients that are most likely already in your pantry. They are the go-to solution for when your mind says, "I want a healthy home-cooked meal," and your body says, "Where's the take-out menu?" With these recipes, you can make amazingly delicious and very quick meals from canned, boxed, and bottled ingredients—from shelf to table in 20 minutes or less.

When you keep a well-stocked pantry, fridge, and freezer, you are only minutes away from a healthy, great-tasting meal, or as I like to call it, "pantry magic."

Before we get to my recipes, I want to talk about the ingredients that either are or should be in your pantry, as well as some tips for pantry cooking. Let's begin with my top ten reasons why you'll want to "cook the pantry."

Ten Reasons to "Cook the Pantry"

Variety: Ingredient components allow you to build meals with great flavor combinations, making for endless variety.

Nutrition: Incorporating nutritious plant-based ingredients such as beans, grains, and vegetables ensures that you eat well-balanced meals.

Economy: Cooking with on-hand ingredients saves you money. When it's easy to whip something up, you're less likely to reach for convenience foods or take-out menus.

Convenience: You can assemble recipes and reheat them later or take them along to eat at work.

Fun: Cooking the pantry can be a creative way to involve your family in eating well. Let them help choose the dinner ingredients.

Flavor: When your pantry is filled with interesting sauces, seasonings, and condiments, you can explore the flavors of the world without leaving your kitchen.

Speed: Because many of the ingredients are ready to eat or already prepared, you can often put together a meal in just minutes.

Peace of mind: With a well-stocked pantry, you will always have the makings of a delicious home-cooked meal.

Simplicity: All you need is a well-stocked pantry and a handful of fresh ingredients to create healthy meals that don't require spending hours in the kitchen.

Entertaining: Create a great meal at short notice when unexpected guests arrive.

Quick-and-Easy Cooking

A pantry that is well-stocked with ingredients to make quick meals can be a real lifesaver when you're short on time and need to get dinner on the table. I developed these recipes so you can cook them in 20 minutes or less to create maximum flavor in the minimum amount of time. As an added bonus, many of the recipes can be made in one pot. This will make short work of both the cooking and the clean-up. For example, in making Pasta with White Beans and Olivada, you'll place the canned beans in a colander to drain, and then dump the cooked pasta over them. Since canned beans are precooked, the hot pasta water will heat the beans and rinse them at the same time. Easy-peasy.

How to Personalize Your Pantry

To make your own "pantry magic," spend a few minutes taking stock of your current larder and fill in with some very handy ingredients you may not have. Your pantry will include nonperishable ingredients (canned, boxed, dried, and bottled), as well as a stash of handy prepared foods that you keep in your freezer. Added to that are long-term items that keep well in the fridge, such as certain condiments, and vegetables that keep for a long time, such as onions, garlic, and potatoes.

The recipes in this book can be made solely from these pantry sources, although, for variety, and because most of us enjoy the flavor and nutrients found in fresh produce, several of the recipes also give you the opportunity to include some.

My pantry list is arranged according to where items are stored (shelf, freezer, refrigerator) and also by the type of ingredient. You don't have to purchase every ingredient on the list. You most likely already have many of them. But as you look the list over, you can tailor it to your taste, your needs, and the area in which you live. Choose the recipes that you like and buy ingredients accordingly.

Rotate Your Stock

Despite their name, nonperishables don't last forever. Many products have expiration dates. Most canned goods, for example, are best used within a year of purchase. As you shop, rotate your pantry goods by placing newer items in the back and moving the older products to the front so you use them first.

The following is a roster of foods and other items to stock up on before you need them. It is meant to augment your regular pantry items such as longer-cooking grains and dried beans. Since everyone's situation is different, use it as a guide in making your own shopping list for ingredients for specific meals that your family will enjoy. Buy only as much as your storage space and budget will allow.

A Well-Stocked Pantry

Any well-stocked plant-based kitchen should include a variety of vegetables, fruits, and herbs; a selection of dried or canned beans; pasta, rice, and other grains; canned tomato products; basic seasonings; nondairy milk, nuts, seeds, and nut butters; as well flours and other standard baking items.

Beyond the basics, you'll want to include particular ingredients for various cuisines that you enjoy. To cook with Mediterranean flavors, for example, stock your shelves with artichoke hearts, olives, roasted red peppers, capers, sun-dried tomatoes, and dried porcini mushrooms. For dishes with an Asian flair, keep flavor enhancers on hand such as tamari, toasted sesame oil, chili paste, sriracha sauce, fresh ginger, rice vinegar, and hoisin sauce.

When you stock your pantry with a variety of international ingredients, you'll always be ready to create meals inspired by your favorite cuisines. Take a tour of your local ethnic markets, where you'll discover culinary treasures that will open up your world to a new realm of creative cooking possibilities. If you don't live near ethnic markets, online shopping puts a global pantry within quick reach.

Pantry List

The following list includes ingredients for a well-stocked vegan pantry. The list is divided into three sections: on the shelf (non-perishables), refrigerator (perishables), and freezer (perishables). You probably already have many of these ingredients on hand, so use this more as a checklist and you'll be able to make any of the recipes in this book—and more. Not included in this list are general pantry items such as dried herbs and spices, flour, cornstarch, and salt.

ON THE SHELF (NON-PERISHABLES)

Proteins

Beans (canned and dried): chickpeas, lentils, white beans, black beans, kidney beans, pinto beans

Nuts and seeds: cashews, pistachios, sesame seeds, pine nuts, walnuts, slivered almonds, sunflower seeds, pumpkin seeds, pecan pieces, roasted peanuts

Soy Curls and/or TVP (texturized vegetable protein)

Grains

quinoa, barley, cornmeal, bulgur, couscous, oats

rice (brown, basmati, jasmine, arborio)

polenta (instant or quick-cooking)

pasta and rice noodles (a variety)

Vegetables

artichoke hearts, canned and/or marinated

capers

chipotles in adobo sauce

giardiniera (Italian pickled vegetables)

hearts of palm

jackfruit, packed in water or brine
olives
roasted red peppers
tomato products (canned: diced, whole, purée, paste; sun-dried: dehydrated or oil-packed)

Sauces and Seasonings
agave nectar
barbecue sauce
chili pastes and sauces: sambal oelek, sriracha, sweet chili sauce
chutney
cocoa
coconut milk, unsweetened (canned)
curry powder and paste
dairy-free chocolate chips
dried chiles
dried fruit: dates, apricots, cranberries, raisins
dried mushrooms
hoisin sauce
instant potato flakes
kimchi
liquid smoke
maple syrup
miso paste
nori/dulse flakes
nutritional yeast
olive oil
panko crumbs
pretzels
rice vinegar
soy sauce: tamari, mushroom sauce (vegan oyster sauce)
tahini
tamarind paste
tapenade
teriyaki sauce
toasted sesame oil

tomato salsa

REFRIGERATOR (PERISHABLES)
almond milk
seitan
tempeh
tofu
vegan sour cream
vegan yogurt

Fresh Produce
asparagus
broccoli
carrots
cauliflower
garlic
ginger
green beans
leafy greens: kale, chard, spinach
lettuce
mushrooms
onions
potatoes
sweet potatoes
tomatoes
winter squash
zucchini

FREEZER (PERISHABLES)
bell pepper strips
breads and dough: pizza dough, puff pastry, phyllo dough, tortillas, flatbreads
chopped spinach
cooked butternut squash
cooked, portioned beans
cooked, portioned rice
shelled edamame
green peas
portioned pesto

Plant Proteins

Shelf-stable ingredients such as beans and dehydrated plant-protein products such as texturized soy protein (TVP) and Soy Curls can come in handy for quick meals.

Beans: Protein-rich beans are inexpensive, easy to prepare, low in fat, and versatile. Popular bean varieties include chickpeas, black-eyed peas, lentils and split peas, black beans, pinto beans, kidney beans, limas, and fava beans, and white beans including Great Northern, navy, and cannellini. If you're using dried beans, they'd need to be cooked up ahead of time before using in these recipes. You can cook dried beans in large batches and then portion and freeze them for ease of use. For convenience, I also suggest keeping a supply of canned beans on hand. Since canned beans usually contain about 1 1/2 cups of beans, home-cooked beans should be portioned and frozen in the same amounts. On average, one pound of dried beans will yield 4 to 6 cups cooked (depending on the bean), or the equivalent of 3 to 4 cans. Beans make a great addition to pasta and grain dishes, as well as vegetable dishes and salads. Beans can be pureed for sauces, dips, and spreads, or mashed to make loaves, burgers, and more. I keep at least two cans each of several varieties on hand as well as some portioned cooked-from-dried beans in the freezer.

Texturized Soy Protein (TVP): This product is made from defatted soy flour and is available in two forms: granular and chunky. A great source of protein, texturized soy protein absorbs flavors well and brings a "meaty" texture to dishes. You can find it in well-stocked supermarkets and natural food stores. It is also available online. The granular-style texturized soy protein can be used to make great chili and tacos or as an addition to spaghetti sauce. The chunky version is good in stews, soups, and stir-fries and can be used instead of beans in many of the recipes in this book: simply place the about 1 cup of texturized soy protein in a heatproof bowl (large enough to allow for expansion) and add enough hot water to cover. Then drain and add to recipes. I personally don't use TVP very often, but since it keeps well, I always have some on the shelf.

Soy Curls: Made by Butler Foods, this great protein product is another dehydrated vegan meat alternative. The "curls" have a great texture, are extremely versatile, and can be used to make fajitas, sandwiches, stir-fries and more. Available in some stores and online, one (8-ounce) package contains approximately 4 1/2 cups. Like texturized soy protein, Soy Curls must be soaked in hot water for 10 minutes to reconstitute. Soy Curls are available online and in specialty food stores, and can't be recommended enough. Since I can't find Soy Curls locally, I order six bags at a time from Amazon.com at a good price. They last a long time and turrn out to be quite economical.

Perishable vegan proteins such as tofu, tempeh, and seitan can be stored for a time in the refrigerator (check their date stamps), and you can also freeze them, although the texture of tofu changes after freezing so it's chewier and more porous.

Tofu: This popular plant protein comes in two types: "Chinese bean curd," which I refer to as "regular" tofu, and silken tofu, or Japanese-style. Both types are available in several textures including soft, firm, and extra-firm. Regular extra-firm tofu is best for stir-fries and other dishes that require a sturdy texture that retains its shape during cooking. Silken tofu is mostly used to make sauces, puddings, or other recipes that call for a smooth and creamy texture. Regular tofu is also sold marinated and baked in a number of flavors, which you can use "as is" without further seasoning. Regular and silken tofu should be treated as being uniquely different from each other — they are not interchangeable in most recipes. Regular tofu needs to be stored unopened in the refrigerator. Once opened, it is best if used right away, although it can be kept in the fridge for several days submerged in fresh water in a covered container to prevent it from absorbing the surrounding flavors. Silken tofu is usually sold in aseptic containers that can be kept unrefrigerated until opened. Once opened, however, it should be used within two to three days. I always have a few containers of extra-firm tofu in the refrigerator since making tofu scrambles is one of our favorite go-to meals. I also like to cut a block of tofu into slabs and marinate and bake it to have on hand for stir-fries.

Can Size

Recipes often call for specific can sizes, but you don't have to be a stickler. For example, if a recipe calls for a 15.5-ounce can, and all you can find is a 16-ouncer, go ahead and use what's available. In most cases, a small amount either way won't make any difference in the outcome.

Tempeh: This versatile plant protein is made from fermented soybeans that are compressed into a cake. Like tofu, tempeh readily absorbs surrounding flavors and is especially suited to hearty stews, stir-fries, and sautés. It marinates well and turns a crisp golden brown when fried. Tempeh is a good source of high-quality soy protein with a chewy meat-like texture. Some varieties of tempeh contain only soy, while others are blended with one or more grains, giving them a mellower flavor. Tempeh is available in refrigerated or freezer section of natural food stores and some supermarkets. Tempeh can be cut lengthwise into thin slices or cut into strips or cubes, or grated. Tempeh must be kept refrigerated where it will keep unopened for several weeks (check the expiration date). Tempeh may also be stored in the freezer. Since my husband isn't a fan of tempeh, you'll rarely find it in my fridge.

Seitan: Also known as "wheat-meat," seitan is made from the protein part of wheat known as gluten. A versatile ingredient with a meaty texture and appearance, it can be sliced thinly and sautéed, diced or cut into strips for stir-fries, stews, and soups, shredded or ground to use like ground beef, or even turned into a roast. If you're looking for an ingredient to win over a meat-eater, this is it. It's easy to make from scratch but can be time-consuming, so it's best to make a large amount at once and freeze the rest in batches. If you don't have the time to make your own, precooked seitan is available in natural food stores, large supermarkets, and Asian markets. My personal favorite brand is Ray's Seitan. It's consistently delicious and used by many vegan restaurants. Since it can be difficult to find in stores, I always stock up when I see it — there are currently five containers of Ray's in my freezer!

Dairy-Free Products

Many brands and varieties of dairy-free milk, including soy, rice, almond, hemp, and oat, are available in shelf-stable aseptic containers that need no refrigeration until they are opened. The 1-quart containers, however, need to be refrigerated once opened. Soy milk and rice milk are also available in a dry powder form that can be reconstituted as needed with water. The recipes in this book can be made with either. Another dairy-free milk option for certain recipes is unsweetened coconut milk, which is available in 13-ounce cans. A staggering variety of plant milks are now available in the refrigerated section of most supermarkets. My personal favorites are unsweetened almond or cashew milk that can be used in both savory and sweet recipes.

There are other convenient dairy-free products I keep on hand. As of this writing, my favorite brand products are Tofutti Better Than Sour Cream, Tofutti Cream Cheese, Chao Cheese Slices, Earth Balance Buttery Spread, and Just Mayo by Hampton Creek.

Vegetable Broth

You may be wondering how to make vegetable broth, since everyone knows a good stock needs at least an hour to cook. Here are some options from your pantry:

- canned broth
- vegetable broth in aseptic containers
- concentrated broth paste in jars
- bouillon cubes
- powdered soup base

When a recipe calls for "2 cups vegetable broth," you can use any of the above items to make it. As with any packaged food, check the ingredients first to make sure it's vegan and also for any additives. (Some of these are high in sodium and contain corn syrup, MSG, and other additives.) A low-sodium organic vegetable broth is best. When using commercial broths, taste them for strength (some have a strong flavor). For a milder broth, you can simply dilute canned broth with water. For example, if a recipe calls for 4 cups of broth, use 1 can (2 cups) of broth plus 2 cups of water. This is also more economical, since some of these broths can be pricey. Another good option (and the one I use the most) is concentrated vegetable broth paste. My favorite brand is Better Than Bouillon vegetarian soup base (available in 8-ounce jars).

The most economical option is vegetable bouillon cubes or powdered soup bases. I like the Vogue Cuisine brand powdered soup bases. They're made with mostly organic ingredients, have a good flavor, no MSG or other additives, and boast reduced sodium. One 12-ounce plastic jar is enough to make 75 cups of broth. Vogue products (and other brands) are available in natural food stores. In addition to using in soups, vegetable broth can be used to "broth sauté" foods (instead of using oil) and can be used instead of plain water to cook grains for added flavor.

In the Fridge and Freezer

Pantry items are not limited by what's on the shelf. It also extends to items that are stored in your refrigerator and freezer. For example, the fridge is where perishable staple foods such as tofu and almond milk are kept as well as open jars and bottles of condiments and sauces.

The freezer is where you can stock up of frozen vegetables such as chopped spinach, green peas, and edamame. I also like to keep a bag of frozen bell pepper strips on hand for stir-fries, as well as cooked rice, beans, seitan, and other foods that can be prepared and divided into meal-sized portions for convenience.

Herbs: Fresh, Dried, and Frozen

Fresh herbs make wonderful additions to our meals, but unless you have your own herb garden, fresh herbs can be expensive and they are highly perishable. The solution is to puree extra fresh herbs (with a little oil, if desired) and freeze them in small quantities, such as a plastic or silicone ice cube tray. That way you have fresh-tasting herbs whenever you need them. If you do not have fresh or fresh-frozen herbs on hand, you can substitute dried for fresh (1 teaspoon of dried = 1 tablespoon of fresh).

Kitchen Time-Savers

One of the main reasons I like to "cook the pantry" is that it's a quick and easy way to get dinner on the table. The most important tip for getting dinner on the table quickly is to keep your pantry well stocked with the ingredients you need to make your favorite recipes. There are lots of other ways to save time in the kitchen. Here are more of my top tips:

Prep the Produce: when you bring home fresh produce from the market, take a few minutes to wash and dry it before you put it away. This will give you a chance to remove wilted leaves and so on as well as to make sure that your ingredients are ready when you need them. Exceptions to this advance prep are berries, mushrooms, and other fragile ingredients that should only be washed just prior to using.

Assemble Ingredients: Gathering your ingredients before you begin cooking will streamline the cooking process. To do this, assemble your *mis en place,* which means gathering the ingredients and equipment you'll need before beginning a recipe. This includes including measuring out the ingredients in advance.

(Re)read the Recipe: When you are familiar with your recipe and you have your ingredients and equipment at hand, you will be amazed at how much more easily you can prepare a meal. Good prep can also help avoid kitchen mishaps, such as missing ingredients, wrong pans, or burning up dinner while you search for a spice or a whisk.

Cook intuitively: Don't be afraid to substitute or change ingredients when it seems appropriate. For example, if you don't like a certain ingredient in a recipe, just make a reasonable substitution for something you do like, such as replacing tarragon with basil or pinto beans with kidney beans. In most cases, the recipe will turn out just as well; maybe better, since it will now have your own personal touch.

Flexibility: What if you find that you're out of an ingredient when you're ready to prepare dinner? While it's best to plan ahead and make sure in advance that you have everything you need in the house, it sometimes it just happens that you run out of an ingredient at the last minute. In those cases, rather than dropping everything to rush out to the store, try to determine whether you have something in the house that can be substituted. To avoid running out of the ingredients you use most frequently, keep an ongoing grocery list in the kitchen so you can write down items the minute you run out or see that you're getting low.

Kitchen Equipment

The type of kitchen equipment needed for pantry cooking tends to be more basic than for other types of cooking. While you can certainly enlist the assistance of small kitchen appliances such as a pressure cooker, slow cooker, or rice steamer, the recipes in this book are made using little more than the usal pots and pans, knives, and mixing bowls. The only special small appliances called for are a food processor and (optionally) a high-speed blender.

You should have at least one pot big enough to boil pasta. A Dutch oven or 4 1/2 to 5-quart pot is ideal for stews, soups, and chili. You will also need a couple of smaller saucepans (a 1 quart and a 2.5 quart), including one with a steamer insert for steaming vegetables. At least two good skillets, ranging in size from 8 inches to 16 inches in diameter, are a must. At least one skillet should have a non-stick surface. All pots and skillets should have lids that fit well.

Other kitchen basics include a few mixing bowls, a set of measuring cups and spoons, a colander, cutting boards, baking dishes and pans, and so on—nothing much beyond these is required to make the recipes in this book.

In addition, there are a few kitchen tools that can help make cooking faster and easier. They include:

- **Blender** — While you can certainly get by with just a food processor for most things, a high-powered blender (such as a VitaMix or BlendTec) is wonderful for making silky-smooth sauces, soups, and anything you want super creamy very quickly. An immersion (or stick) blender can also come in handy, if you have one.

- **Box grater** — Use a box grater to grate or shred a small amount of food such as citrus zest or cabbage (save the food processor for larger amounts). For extra-small jobs, use a microplane grater.

- **Food processor** — A food processor is essential for making pesto, pureeing vegetables, chopping nuts, and making bread crumbs. It is also great for making pie dough, chopping vegetables, and numerous other mixing and chopping tasks. The trick is to know when it will be faster to cut, whisk, or chop by hand, and that can usually be determined by the quantity of food involved. In addition to a large capacity processor, some people also have a smaller model that they use for smaller tasks.

- **Knives** — The three most essential knives are a paring knife for peeling and trimming, a long serrated knife for slicing bread or tomatoes, and a good chef's knife (8 to 10 inches) for virtually everything else. Buy the best quality knives you can afford and keep them sharp. You can chop more quickly and safely with sharp knives than dull ones.

- **Microwave** —It's ideal when you need a small amount of melted chocolate or a hot liquid. You can use it to soften hard winter squashes to make them easier to cut.

- **Salad spinner** — The easiest and quickest way to dry your salad greens after washing them. No more laying out individual lettuce leaves to dry on paper towels. This thing really works great to get every drop of water off your lettuce so it's crisp and ready for your salad.

- **Vegetable peeler** — This low-tech gadget is great for peeling carrots, potatoes, cucumbers, and so on. It can also be used to cut zucchini into "pasta" ribbons.

About the Recipes

Pantry cooking is about more than just convenience; it is also about resourcefulness. Keeping a well-stocked pantry means that you will always have the ingredients on hand to make a satisfying meal.

The recipes in this book have been designed for simple and speedy preparation relying mostly on your pantry and freezer along with carefully chosen fresh ingredients. These recipes can help you enjoy a plant-based diet without a lot of extra time and effort.

Whether you start with pantry staples that you bought from a store or ones that you made in advance from scratch, you'll love the versatility, variety, and nutrition in these recipes that take twenty minutes or less of active time to prepare.

Note: Not included in the twenty minutes are advance soaking times, chilling times, or other steps that do not require active cooking time.

2

Soups
Stews
and
Chilis

Chipotle Corn Chowder 14

White Beans and Greens Soup 16

Hot and Sour Noodle Soup 17

Tortilla Soup 18

Pretty Good Gumbo 19

Minestrone Soup 21

Black Bean Soup with a Whisper of Sherry 22

Shiitake Happens Mushroom Soup 23

Curry-Spiced Pumpkin Bisque 24

Creamy Peanut Soup 25

Everyone's Favorite Black Bean Chili 26

Pantry Plus Gazpacho 28

Vegetable Bricolage 29

Moroccan-Spiced Vegetable Stew 30

Red Bean Chili 31

Chana Masala 32

Chipotle Corn Chowder

This sweet, satisfying chowder is made with a canned whole kernel corn. The garnish of pimientos and parsley adds a dash of color.

1 tablespoon safflower oil
1 medium onion, minced or shredded
1 carrot, finely chopped or shredded
1 russet potato, finely chopped or shredded
1/4 teaspoon celery salt
2 cups vegetable broth
1 (16-ounce) bag frozen corn kernels
Salt and ground black pepper
1/2 teaspoon ground coriander
1/2 teaspoon liquid smoke
2 cups plain unsweetened almond milk
1/2 cup raw cashew pieces, soaked for 3 hours, then drained
1 chipotle chile in adobo sauce
2 tablespoons minced fresh parsley
1 (2-ounce) jar chopped pimientos, drained

Heat the oil in a large saucepan over medium heat. Add the onion, carrot, and potato. Cover and cook for 4 minutes to soften. Stir in the celery salt, broth, corn, and salt and pepper to taste. Bring to a boil, then reduce the heat to a simmer, stir in the coriander, liquid smoke, and almond milk, and cook, stirring frequently, for 5 minutes.

While the soup is simmering, combine the drained cashews and chipotle in a blender with 1 cup of the simmering broth from the soup. Blend until smooth and creamy, then add 1 more cup of the soup and blend until smooth. Stir the mixture back into the soup. Taste and adjust the seasonings. Ladle the soup into bowls and garnish with parsley and pimientos.

MAKES 4 SERVINGS

White Beans and Greens Soup

This homey soup makes a hearty and economical main dish. Stellini, the small star-shaped pasta, add a touch of whimsy, but you can substitute another small soup pasta, such as acine de pepe or pastene (or even ramen).

1 tablespoon olive oil
1 yellow onion, minced
3 garlic cloves, minced
4 cups vegetable broth
1 (16-ounce) can cannellini beans, drained
1/2 teaspoon dried marjoram
1/4 teaspoon dried savory
1/4 teaspoon red pepper flakes
Salt and black pepper
1/4 cup stellini or other small soup pasta
1 (10-ounce) package frozen spinach, thawed and squeezed dry

Heat the oil in a large pot over medium heat. Add the onion and cook for 5 minutes to soften. Add the garlic and cook until fragrant, 30 seconds. Stir in the broth, beans, marjoram, savory, red pepper flakes, and salt and pepper to taste. Bring to a boil and cook for 5 minutes, then stir in the pasta and spinach, reduce the heat to a simmer and cook until the pasta is tender, 5 to 8 minutes (depending on the type of pasta). Serve hot.

MAKES 4 SERVINGS

Hot and Sour Noodle Soup

With this soup, you get spicy, pungent, delicious, and soothing all in one bowl. It's also a great way to use those dried mushrooms and that can of bamboo shoots sitting in your pantry. If you prefer to use fresh sliced mushrooms, add them when you add the garlic and proceed with the recipe.

1/4 ounce dried cloud ear mushrooms or 1 (8-ounce) can straw mushrooms, drained
1 tablespoon safflower oil
2 garlic cloves, minced
1 tablespoon grated ginger
4 cups vegetable broth
3 tablespoons tamari soy sauce
2 tablespoons rice vinegar
1/2 teaspoon sugar
1 teaspoon Asian chili paste
1 (8-ounce) can bamboo shoots, drained and cut into julienne strips
2 teaspoons cornstarch dissolved in 1 tablespoon water
14-ounces extra-firm tofu, diced
1 teaspoon toasted sesame oil
1 teaspoon Asian chili oil
3 scallions, chopped

If using dried mushrooms, soak them in a bowl of hot water until softened. Drain and cut into julienne strips and set aside.

Heat the safflower oil in a large saucepan over medium heat. Add the garlic and ginger and cook until fragrant, about 30 seconds. Add the vegetable broth, tamari, vinegar, sugar, chili paste, bamboo shoots, and the reserved mushrooms. Bring to a boil over high heat, then reduce the heat to a simmer and cook over medium heat for 5 minutes to allow the flavors to combine. Add the cornstarch mixture, stirring to thicken slightly. Add the tofu, sesame oil, chili oil, and scallions, and cook until heated through, about 5 minutes.

MAKES 4 SERVINGS

Tortilla Soup

Crushed tortilla chips and a jar of tomato salsa are key to getting this soup on the table in just minutes. I like to add reconstituted Soy Curls for heartiness and texture, but you can leave them out if you like or substitute a cup or two of diced seitan. Serve with a bowl of tortilla chips on the table for those who want to add a few extra to their soup.

1 tablespoon olive oil
3 garlic cloves, minced
1 teaspoon chili powder
1 (24-ounce) jar chunky tomato salsa (mild or hot)
2 (15.5-ounce) cans black beans, rinsed and drained
1 cup Soy Curls (reconstituted in hot water for 10 minutes)
1 can diced tomatoes with green chiles, undrained
1 1/2 cups frozen corn kernels
1 cup water or vegetable broth
Salt and ground black pepper
2 scallions, minced
1 cup crushed tortilla chips
2 tablespoons chopped fresh cilantro
1 tablespoon fresh lime juice
1 ripe Hass avocado, peeled, pitted, and diced

Heat the oil in a large pot over medium heat. Add the garlic and cook until fragrant, 30 seconds. Stir in the chili powder, then add the salsa, beans, Soy Curls, tomatoes and their juice, corn, and water. Season to taste with salt and pepper. Bring to a boil, then reduce the heat to a simmer and cook for 5 minutes. Add the scallions, the crushed tortilla chips, and cilantro and cook for 2 minutes longer. Remove from the heat and stir in the lime juice, then taste and adjust the seasonings, if needed. Serve hot topped with avocado.

MAKES 4 SERVINGS

Pretty Good Gumbo

The name of this spicy Cajun soup means "okra," although some people may choose not to include the mucilaginous vegetable when they make the soup. The optional filé powder is made from ground sassafras leaves and is available at gourmet grocers or online. If you don't have quick-cooking rice on hand, add a cup or more of fresh or frozen cooked rice.

1 tablespoon olive oil
1 medium onion, minced
3 garlic cloves, minced
1 (14.5-ounce) can diced fire-roasted tomatoes, undrained
1 (6-ounce) jar roasted red bell pepper, diced
5 cups vegetable broth
1 (15.5-ounce) can dark red kidney beans, drained
1/2 cup quick-cooking brown rice
1 1/2 cups frozen sliced okra (optional)
1 teaspoon dried thyme
1 teaspoon filé powder (optional)
1/2 teaspoon cayenne
1/4 teaspoon celery salt
Salt and ground black pepper
1 teaspoon Tabasco, or to taste

Heat the oil in a large pot over medium heat. Add the onion and cook for 5 minutes to soften. Add the garlic and cook until fragrant, 30 seconds. Stir in the tomatoes, bell pepper, and broth and bring to a boil. Reduce heat to low and add the beans, rice, okra (if using), thyme, file powder (if using), cayenne, celery salt, and salt and pepper to taste. Simmer, stirring occasionally for 10 minutes or until the rice and vegetables are tender and the soup is hot. Add the Tabasco and taste to adjust the seasonings. Serve hot.

MAKES 4 SERVINGS

Minestrone Soup

The classic Italian vegetable soup typically includes a wide variety of vegetables. Use up any fresh veggies or herbs you may have on hand or use frozen vegetables. Mix and match according to your own taste. The key to a quicker cooking time is to cut the fresh vegetables as thin as possible. For a heartier soup, just before serving, stir in some cooked pasta, rice, or other grains.

1 tablespoon olive oil
1 medium onion, finely chopped
3 garlic cloves, minced
4 cups fresh or frozen chopped vegetables (such as carrots, kale, green beans, zucchini, in any combination)
1 (15.5-ounce) can chickpeas or white beans, drained
1 (14.5 ounce) can diced fire-roasted tomatoes, undrained
4 cups vegetable broth
1 teaspoon dried basil
1/2 teaspoon dried oregano
2 tablespoons chopped fresh parsley
Salt and black pepper
1 1/2 cups cooked pasta, rice, or other grain (optional)

Heat the oil in a large saucepan over medium heat. Add the onion and cook for 5 minutes to soften. Add the garlic and cook until fragrant, 30 seconds. Stir in the vegetables, tomatoes, chickpeas, and broth Season with basil, oregano, parsley, and salt and pepper to taste. Bring to a boil, then reduce heat to low and simmer 15 minutes or until the vegetables are tender. Stir in the pasta or grain, if using. Taste and adjust the seasonings, if needed.

MAKES 4 SERVINGS

Black Bean Soup with a Whisper of Sherry

This satisfying soup is substantial enough to serve as a main course. Serve it with a salad and some crackers or toasted bread for some crunch-appeal. To make it creamier, use a stick blender to purée a portion of the soup right in the pot, or transfer a few cups of soup to a blender to purée then return it to the pot. Use hot green chiles instead of mild if you want a bit of heat.

> 1 tablespoon olive oil
> 1 medium onion, minced
> 1 large carrot, finely chopped
> 3 garlic cloves, minced
> 1 teaspoon dried oregano
> 1/2 teaspoon ground cumin
> 2 (15.5-ounce) cans black beans, drained
> 1 (14.5-ounce) can diced fire-roasted tomatoes, undrained
> 1 (4-ounce) can chopped mild green chiles, drained
> 3 cups vegetable broth or water
> 1/4 teaspoon celery salt, or to taste
> Black pepper
> 2 tablespoons dry sherry

Heat the oil in a large pot over medium heat. Add the onion and carrot and cook for 5 minutes to soften. Add the garlic, and cook until fragrant, 30 seconds. Stir in the oregano and cumin, then add the black beans, tomatoes, and chiles. Add the broth and season with celery salt and pepper to taste. Simmer for 15 minutes to heat through and allow flavors to develop. Just before serving, stir in the sherry.

MAKES 4 SERVINGS

Shiitake Happens Mushroom Soup

Mushroom lovers will savor the rich flavor created by using shiitakes three ways, fresh, dried, and jarred. If you prefer using all fresh mushrooms, double up on the fresh shiitakes or add some other type of mushroom along with the shiitakes. To make this soup a meal, add a can of white beans.

- 1/4 ounce dried shiitake mushrooms
- 1 tablespoon olive oil
- 1 medium onion, minced
- 3 garlic cloves, minced
- 8 ounces fresh shiitake mushrooms, stemmed and sliced
- 3 tablespoons dry sherry
- 1 teaspoon dried thyme
- 4 cups vegetable broth
- 1/2 cup quick-cooking brown or white rice
- 1 (8-ounce) jar sliced shiitake mushrooms, drained
- 2 tablespoons minced fresh parsley or dill
- 1/4 teaspoon celery salt
- 1/4 teaspoon black pepper

Soak the dried mushrooms in enough hot water to cover until softened. Thinly slice the mushrooms and set them aside. Save the soaking water.

Heat the oil in a large pot over medium heat. Add the onion and cook for 5 minutes to soften. Add the garlic and fresh shiitakes and cook for 30 seconds, then stir in the sherry and thyme, and cook 1 minute longer.

Add the soaked dried mushrooms to the pot along with the broth and 1/2 cup of the mushroom soaking water and bring to a boil. Reduce heat to low, add the rice, jarred shiitakes, parsley, celery salt, and pepper. Simmer for 10 minutes. Taste to adjust seasonings.

MAKES 4 SERVINGS

Curry-Spiced Pumpkin Bisque

If you like the flavor combination of curry and pumpkin, you'll love this soup. Enjoy as is for a creamy soup, or add some cooked vegetables and chickpeas and serve over rice for a hearty meal.

1 (15-ounce) can pumpkin purée
1 tablespoon curry powder
1 teaspoon light brown sugar
1 teaspoon ground coriander
1/2 teaspoon ground cumin
1 (13.5-ounce) can unsweetened coconut milk
1 1/2 cups vegetable broth or water
Salt and black pepper
2 tablespoons pumpkin seeds (optional garnish)

Combine the pumpkin, curry powder, brown sugar, coriander, and cumin in a pot over medium heat. Whisk in the coconut milk a little at a time until smooth. Stir in the vegetable broth, then season with salt and pepper, to taste. Simmer for 10 minutes to allow flavors to develop, stirring occasionally. Taste to adjust seasonings and serve hot, garnished with pumpkin seeds, if desired.

MAKES 4 SERVINGS

Creamy Peanut Soup

The secret ingredient in this rich, creamy peanut soup is the instant potato flakes. Look for dehydrated instant potato flakes with no additives, such as Bob's Red Mill brand, in which the only ingredient is dehydrated potatoes. The flavor of this easy and delicious soul can be altered to suit your mood. Feel like a Thai peanut soup? Add a smidge of lime juice, soy sauce, and chili paste. For an Indian flair, stir in some curry powder. Or to simply jazz it up, add fresh or dried herb of choice.

- 4 cups vegetable broth or water
- 1 cup instant potato flakes
- 1/2 cup creamy peanut butter
- 1/4 teaspoon celery salt
- 1/8 teaspoon onion powder
- Black pepper
- 1/4 cup chopped dry-roasted peanuts

Bring the broth to a boil in a large pot. Stir in the potato flakes until well blended. Reduce the heat to low. Place the peanut butter in a bowl and whisk in 1 cup of the hot broth mixture, blending until smooth. Stir the peanut butter mixture into the saucepan and add the celery salt, onion powder, and pepper to taste. Simmer 5 minutes to heat through and blend flavors. Serve sprinkled with the chopped peanuts.

MAKES 4 SERVINGS

Everyone's Favorite Black Bean Chili

This is my go-to chili recipe. If I have cooked lentils on hand, I use them instead of the Soy Curls. You can also add some dark red kidney beans, if you like, to change things up a bit. If using Soy Curls, place them in a heatproof bowl with enough hot water to cover and set aside for 10 minutes to reconstitute.

1 cup reconstituted crumbled Soy Curls or texturized soy protein granules (optional)
2 (15.5-ounce) cans black beans, drained
1 (24-ounce) jar chunky tomato salsa (hot or mild)
1/4 cup bottled barbecue sauce
2 tablespoons chili powder, or to taste
1 teaspoon dried oregano
1/2 teaspoon ground cumin
Salt and ground black pepper, to taste
1 1/2 cups frozen corn kernels, thawed
Water, as needed

Combine the ingredients (including the reconstituted Soy Curls, if using) in a saucepan, reserving 1/2 cup of the corn. Cover and cook over medium heat, stirring occasionally, until heated through and the flavors are well blended. Add as much water as needed to create a sauce and prevent sticking to the bottom of the pan.

Reduce heat to medium and simmer, stirring frequently, until heated through and long enough to cook off any raw taste from the chili powder, about 15 minutes. Garnish with the remaining corn kernels.

MAKES 4 SERVINGS

Pantry Plus Gazpacho

If you're craving gazpacho, but fresh tomatoes are out of season, try this almost-instant pantry version of the famous "salad soup." To serve it as a main dish, just add a can of drained chickpeas or pinto beans. Feel free to add in chopped fresh cucumber, bell pepper, or other fresh veggies, if you have them on hand.

1 (14.5-ounce) can diced tomatoes, finely chopped
1 (4-ounce) jar roasted red peppers, chopped
1 (4-ounce) can chopped mild green chiles, drained
2 tablespoons chopped capers
2 scallions, finely minced
1 garlic clove, finely minced
1 tablespoon olive oil
1 tablespoon red wine vinegar
3 cups tomato or blended vegetable juice (such as V8)
1/2 teaspoon celery salt
2 tablespoons minced fresh parsley
1 teaspoon Tabasco sauce

Combine all of the ingredients in a large bowl. Cover and refrigerate for a few hours to chill.

Serve chilled with Tabasco on the side for those who like an extra jolt of heat.

MAKES 4 SERVINGS

Vegetable Bricolage

This is the stew you make when you're down to your last bits of produce and grocery day isn't until tomorrow. Adapt this recipe according to what you have on hand, which is how I came up with the name of this recipe since the term bricolage is from the French for "tinkering." It means the creation of something from several on-hand items. So you can call this a "stew made from odds and ends," but I think "bricolage" sounds a lot more intriguing. If you have cooked vegetables or grains on hand, add them just before serving.

1 tablespoon olive oil
1 yellow onion, finely chopped
1 large carrot, thinly sliced
3 garlic cloves, minced
1 teaspoon dried basil
1/2 teaspoon dried oregano
2 (15.5-ounce) cans white beans, drained
1 (14.5-ounce) can petite diced tomatoes, undrained
1 1/2 cups vegetable broth
Salt and black pepper
10 ounces frozen chopped spinach, thawed and squeezed dry

Heat the oil in a large pot over medium heat. Add the onion, carrot, garlic, basil, and oregano. Cover and cook, stirring occasionally, until vegetables soften, about 5 minutes.

Add the beans, tomatoes, broth, and salt and pepper to taste, and bring to a boil. Reduce the heat to a simmer, cover, and cook for 10 minutes. Stir in the spinach and simmer until the vegetables are tender, about 5 minutes longer. Taste and adjust the seasonings, if needed. Serve hot.

MAKES 4 SERVINGS

Moroccan-Spiced Vegetable Stew

Fragrant spices and dried fruits lend a Moroccan flavor to this hearty stew that just begs to be served over couscous, freekeh, or quinoa to absorb the delicious flavors.

1 tablespoon olive oil
1 medium onion, finely chopped
1 carrot, thinly sliced
2 garlic cloves, minced
1 teaspoon ground cumin
1 teaspoon ground coriander
1/2 teaspoon ground cinnamon
1 (14.5-ounce) can diced tomatoes, drained
1 (15.5-ounce) can chickpeas, drained
1 1/4 cups vegetable broth
1 1/2 cups frozen cut green beans, thawed
1/2 cup dried mixed fruit or dried apricots and raisins
Salt and black pepper
1/2 cup frozen green peas, thawed

In a large saucepan, heat the oil over medium heat. Add the onion and carrot and cook for 5 minutes to soften. Add the garlic, cumin, coriander, and cinnamon and cook, stirring, for 30 seconds. Add the tomatoes, chickpeas, and broth and bring to a boil.

Reduce the heat to low, add the green beans and dried fruit. Season to taste with salt and pepper and simmer, stirring occasionally, until the vegetables are tender, about 10 minutes. Taste and adjust the seasonings, if needed. Stir in the peas and cook 3 minutes longer to heat through.

MAKES 4 SERVINGS

Red Bean Chili

If not using the optional TVP, add the third can of red beans or crumbled Soy Curls. This recipe used frozen onion and bell pepper strips to save time, and can be economical, too, given the price of fresh red or yellow bell peppers. Serve the chili with crackers or cornbread, or ladle it over rice or noodles.

1 cup texturized vegetable protein granules (TVP), (optional)
2 (14.5-ounce) cans fire-roasted diced tomatoes, undrained
1 1/2 cups frozen onion and bell pepper strips, partially thawed and chopped
2 or 3 (15.5-ounce) cans kidney beans, drained
2 to 3 tablespoons chili powder
1 chipotle chile in adobo, minced
Salt and black pepper

If using TVP, place it in a heatproof bowl with enough hot water to cover and set aside for 5 minutes to reconstitute. Combine all the ingredients in a large pot over medium heat, stirring to blend. Bring just to a boil, then reduce the heat to a simmer, and cook, stirring occasionally, until flavors are blended, about 15 minutes. Taste to adjust seasonings. Serve hot.

MAKES 4 SERVINGS

Chana Masala

One of my favorite Indian dishes is the classic chickpea and tomato dish known as chana masala. This easy but flavorful version can be enjoyed with warm naan or served over rice.

1 tablespoon safflower oil
1 small yellow onion, minced
3 garlic cloves, pressed or minced
1 tablespoon grated fresh ginger
1 hot green chile, seeded and minced
2 teaspoons garam masala
1 teaspoon ground coriander
1/2 teaspoon ground cumin
1/2 teaspoon turmeric
1 teaspoon salt
1/4 teaspoon ground black pepper
2 (14.5-ounce) cans fire-roasted diced tomatoes, undrained
2 (15.5 ounce) cans chickpeas, rinsed and drained
Hot cooked rice, to serve
Chopped cilantro, for garnish

Heat the oil in a large pot over medium heat. Add the onion and cook until softened, 4 minutes. Add the garlic, ginger, and chile, and cook, stirring, for 1 minute longer. Stir in the garam masala, coriander, cumin, turmeric, salt, and pepper. Stir in the tomatoes and chickpeas bring to a boil. Reduce the heat to a simmer and cook for 10 minutes to blend the flavors. Use a stick blender or potato masher to mash some of the chickpeas right in the pot, then stir to blend. Serve hot over rice. Garnish with cilantro.

MAKES 4 SERVINGS

3

Salad Savvy

Hearts of Palm Ceviche 36

Five-Minute Couscous Salad 38

Amazing Technicolor Chickpea Salad 39

Moroccan Couscous Salad 40

Tabbouleh Salad 41

Pantry Pasta Salad 42

Taco Salad with Corn and Black Bean Salsa 45

Composed Marinated Vegetable Salad 46

Nutty Ramen Salad 47

Pinto Bean and Corn Salad 48

Southwest Salmagundi 49

Three's-a-Crowd Bean Salad 51

White Bean Niçoise Salad 52

Asian Noodle Salad with Peanut Dressing 53

Suddenly Sushi Salad 54

Sesame Soba Salad 57

Zucchini "Pasta" Salad 58

Asian Noodle Slaw 59

Avocado Goddess Potato Salad 60

Three-Tomato Pasta Salad 61

Hearts of Palm Ceviche

Hearts of palm stand in for raw fish in this plant-powered version of the classic South American dish. There are many versions of this salad throughout central and South America, so let's add this plant-based pantry version to the list. If you like heat, add the jalapeño – if not, leave it out. The avocado is an optional but delicious inclusion. I especially like to serve this salad as an appetizer with tortilla chips or over shredded lettuce.

1/4 cup fresh lime juice
2 tablespoons olive oil
1 jalapeño, seeded and minced (optional)
1/2 teaspoon sugar
2 tablespoons minced scallion or onion
1 teaspoon small capers
Salt and ground black pepper
1/2 English cucumber, peeled and thinly sliced
1 (14-ounce) jar hearts of palm, cut into 1/4-inch rounds
1 medium tomato, finely chopped or 1 (4-ounce) jar chopped pimientos
2 tablespoons kalamata olives or green olives, pitted and halved
2 tablespoons chopped fresh cilantro or parsley
1 ripe avocado, peeled, pitted and diced (optional)
Tortilla chips, to serve

In a small bowl, combine the lime juice, oil, jalapeño, if using, sugar, scallions, capers, and salt and pepper to taste. Mix well.

In a large shallow bowl arrange the cucumber slices in a layer. Top with a layer of the hearts of palm slices. Sprinkle the tomato and olives, then drizzle with the reserved dressing. Set aside to marinate at room temperature for 15 minutes or refrigerate for up to 3 hours before serving. When ready to serve, taste and adjust the seasonings if needed and sprinkle with the cilantro and avocado if using. Serve with tortilla chips.

MAKES 4 SERVINGS

Five-Minute Couscous Salad

Couscous is ideal for quick pantry cooking. Unlike some grains which can take up to an hour to cook, couscous takes just five minutes. Be sure to stock up on the whole-grain variety for optimum nutrition. As is, the recipe is a main-dish salad for four, but can be easily halved for two. This salad employs jarred three-bean salad for the ultimate in pantry convenience, but you can, instead, use any combination of vegetables you may have on hand (steamed broccoli with white beans, diced cucumbers, and tomatoes is a good combination) -- just toss them with a little vinaigrette before using.

   2 1/2 cups water
   1 vegetable bouillon cube or 1 teaspoon vegetable soup base
   2 cups whole-grain couscous
   1/2 cup slivered almonds, lightly toasted
   2 tablespoons fresh parsley
   1 tablespoon olive oil
   1 tablespoon rice vinegar
   1/8 teaspoon sugar
   2 teaspoons dried minced chives
   Salt and black pepper
   2 (16-ounce) jars three-bean salad, drained

In a saucepan, combine the water and bouillon cube, and bring to a boil. Stir in the couscous, cover the saucepan, and remove it from the heat. Let the mixture stand for 5 minutes. Stir in the almonds, parsley, oil, vinegar, sugar, chives, and salt and pepper to taste. Mix well. Mound the couscous mixture in the center of a large shallow bowl or platter or individual shallow bowls and spoon the three-bean salad around the couscous

MAKES 4 SERVINGS

Amazing Technicolor Chickpea Salad

When you need a bite of something to make you smile, try this salad. A combination of chickpeas, beets, and pineapple, it may seem like an unusual trio but it delivers good nutrition while lighting up your taste buds. If you have fresh pineapple or fresh roasted beets to use instead of jarred, that will make this salad all the better.

1 (8-ounce) jar sliced beets, drained
1 (15-ounce) can chickpeas, drained
1 (8-ounce) can chunk pineapple, drained with juice reserved
1 tablespoon olive oil
1 teaspoon lemon juice
1/4 teaspoon sugar
Salt and black pepper
Salad greens, to serve (optional)

Cut the beets into 1/4-inch dice and transfer to a medium bowl. Add the chickpeas, and pineapple chunks. Drizzle on about 1/3 cup of the reserved pineapple juice, the oil, lemon juice, and sugar. Season with salt and pepper, and mix well. Serve over lettuce, if using.

MAKES 4 SERVINGS

Moroccan Couscous Salad

Fragrant spices make this salad the one to choose when you want something that will add fun to the routine. Brimming with a variety of flavors and textures, it takes only a few minutes to prepare. Quinoa, freekeh, or long-grain brown rice may be used instead of the couscous, but they will have longer cooking times.

1 tablespoon olive oil
3/4 teaspoon ground coriander
1/4 teaspoon ground ginger
1/4 teaspoon ground cinnamon
1/4 teaspoon ground cumin
1/4 teaspoon ground turmeric
1/4 teaspoon cayenne
1 1/2 cups couscous
1 large carrot, finely shredded
1 1/4 cups water
1 cup apple juice
1 teaspoon light brown sugar
Salt
2 scallions, minced
1 (15.5-ounce) can chickpeas, drained
1/4 cup chopped dried fruit
1/4 cup golden raisins
Salad greens, to serve (optional)
2 tablespoons chopped unsalted peanuts or other nuts

Heat 1/2 tablespoon of the oil in a medium saucepan over low heat. Add the coriander, ginger, cinnamon, cumin, turmeric, cayenne, and couscous and stir until fragrant, about 1 minute. Do not burn. Stir in the carrot, water, and juice, and bring to a boil. Reduce the heat to very low, cover and cook 5 minutes. Remove from the heat and let stand about 5 minutes longer.

Transfer the couscous to a large bowl, using a fork to fluff it up. Stir in the remaining 1/2 tablespoon of oil, the sugar, and salt to taste. Add the scallions, chickpeas, dried fruit, and raisins. Toss gently to combine. Serve over salad greens, if using. Garnish with peanuts.

MAKES 4 SERVINGS

Tabbouleh Salad

Traditionally made with bulgur and lots of fresh parsley and tomatoes, tabbouleh is best when fresh tomatoes are at their peak. For those times when good tomatoes are scarce, here's a way to enjoy this hearty and nourishing salad. (If fresh tomatoes are available, substitute 1 1/2 cups diced fresh tomatoes for the canned.)

2 cups water
1 cup medium-grind bulgur
1 (14.5-ounce) can petite diced tomatoes, well-drained
1 (15.5-ounce) can chickpeas, drained
1/4 cup chopped fresh parsley
2 tablespoons minced red onion or scallions
1 tablespoon chopped fresh mint or 1 teaspoon dried mint
1/4 cup olive oil
2 tablespoons fresh lemon juice
Salt and black pepper

Bring the water to a boil in a saucepan and add the bulgur. Reduce the heat to low, cover, and simmer for 15 minutes, or until the water is absorbed. Drain any remaining water and blot the bulgur to remove excess moisture. Place the bulgur in a bowl and allow to cool. Add the tomatoes, chickpeas, parsley, onion, and mint. Drizzle on the oil, lemon juice, and salt and pepper to taste. Toss well to combine.

MAKES 4 SERVINGS

Pantry Pasta Salad

The great thing about this recipe is that the portion size is easy to adjust. This version makes four average servings, or enough for two or three hungry eaters. To increase the volume, cook an entire pound of pasta and add additional pantry goodies, such as olives, roasted red peppers, or pine nuts. You can also add fresh vegetables and herbs (see optional additions).

8 ounces bite-sized pasta of choice
1 (15.5-ounce) can cannellini beans or chickpeas, drained
1 (6-ounce) jar marinated artichoke hearts, drained
1 6-ounce) jar roasted red bell peppers
1/2 cup thawed frozen baby peas
1/3 cup kalamata olives, pitted and halved
3 sun-dried tomatoes (oil-packed or reconstituted dried), cut into thin strips
2 teaspoons capers, drained
3 tablespoons olive oil
2 tablespoons lemon juice
1 teaspoon agave nectar
1 or 2 garlic cloves, pressed
1 teaspoon dried basil
1/2 teaspoon dried oregano
Salt and ground black pepper
Optional additions: halved cherry or grape tomatoes, minced red onion, chopped scallions, chopped celery, grated carrot, leftover cooked or steamed veggies such as broccoli or green beans, chopped fresh parsley or basil

Cook the pasta in a pot of boiling salted water until it is al dente. Drain and run under cold water, then drain again and transfer to a large bowl. Add the beans, artichokes, bell peppers, peas, olives, sun-dried tomatoes, and capers. Toss gently to combine. Set aside.

In a small bowl, combine the olive oil, lemon juice, agave, garlic, basil, oregano, and salt and pepper to taste. Stir well to break up and distribute the garlic. Pour the dressing over the pasta salad. Add any optional add-ins and toss to combine. Taste and adjust the seasonings, if needed.

MAKES 4 SERVINGS

Taco Salad with Corn and Black Bean Salsa

This recipe combines pantry ingredients to make a luscious main dish salad. If you don't have lettuce, cilantro, or an avocado on hand, it's still quite tasty without them.

1 (16-ounce) jar tomato salsa (mild or hot)
1 (15-ounce) can black beans, drained and rinsed
1 cup frozen corn kernels, steamed or 1 (8-ounce) can corn kernels, drained
1/4 cup chopped scallions
1/4 cup chopped fresh cilantro
4 cups coarsely chopped romaine lettuce
1 1/2 cups chopped plum tomatoes (or more tomato salsa)
2 cups tortilla chips, plus more to serve
1 ripe Hass avocado, peeled, pitted, and chopped
1/2 cup vegan sour cream, optional
1 cup shredded vegan cheddar cheese, optional

In a bowl, combine the salsa, beans, and corn. Stir in the scallions and cilantro and mix well.

Divide the lettuce equally among four shallow bowls. Top equally with the black bean mixture. Top each serving with the tomato, chips, avocado, and sour cream and/or cheese, if using.

MAKES 4 SERVINGS

Composed Marinated Vegetable Salad

Despite its humble origins in your pantry hoard, this salad draws its inspiration both from a French salade composé and an Italian antipasto, wherein you artfully arrange the salad components on a platter.

    2 tablespoons olive oil
    1 1/2 tablespoons balsamic vinegar
    1 teaspoon minced garlic
    1/2 teaspoon sugar
    1/2 teaspoon dried basil
    Salt and black pepper
    3 cups shredded Romaine lettuce (optional)
    2 cups fresh or frozen cut green beans, steamed
    1 (6-ounce) jar roasted red bell pepper, drained and cut into strips
    1 (15.5-ounce) can cannellini beans, drained and rinsed
    1 (6-ounce) jar marinated artichoke hearts, drained
    1/4 cup pitted kalamata olives, cut in half
    2 tablespoons toasted pine nuts, walnut pieces, or slivered almonds

In a small bowl combine the olive oil, balsamic vinegar, garlic, sugar, basil, salt, and pepper. Whisk to combine. Set aside.

If using lettuce, spread it evenly on a large platter or shallow bowl. Arrange the green beans, bell peppers, cannellini beans, and artichoke hearts on top in separate piles. Drizzle the reserved dressing evenly over all. Nestle the olives decoratively among the vegetables. Sprinkle with pine nuts and serve.

MAKES 4 SERVINGS

Nutty Ramen Salad

This may sound nutty, but ramen noodles can be used to make a great salad. And, with the addition of slivered almonds, it even tastes nutty. As always, toss out the seasoning packets that come with the ramen noodles. For a heartier salad, add whatever vegetables you may have on hand such as red bell pepper or steamed broccoli, or some diced baked tofu.

2 ramen noodle bricks, broken up into 1-inch pieces
1 tablespoon dehydrated onion
1 large carrot, shredded
1 cup chopped celery
1 tablespoon safflower oil
1 cup slivered almonds
1/4 cup sunflower seeds
3 tablespoons sesame seeds
2 tablespoons rice wine vinegar
2 teaspoons toasted sesame oil
1 teaspoon sugar
1/4 teaspoon salt
1/4 teaspoon garlic powder
1/4 teaspoon cayenne (optional)
1 tablespoon tamari or other soy sauce

Place the noodles in a small saucepan with enough boiling water to cover. Reduce heat to low and simmer for 1 minute. Drain the noodles well in a colander, then transfer to a bowl. Add the carrots and celery and set aside.

Heat the safflower oil in a skillet over medium heat. Add the almonds and cook, stirring, until golden, 3 to 5 minutes. Add the sunflower seeds and sesame seeds and continue to cook until sesame seeds turn golden brown, 1 to 2 minutes longer. Add the seeds to the noodle mixture and toss to combine.

Add the vinegar, sesame oil, sugar, salt, garlic powder, cayenne (if using), and tamari, tossing well to coat. Cover and let stand for 10 minutes before serving.

MAKES 4 SERVINGS

Pinto Bean and Corn Salad

This main dish salad is great alone or on a bed of lettuce and topped with diced avocado. It's also good heated and served over rice.

- 2 cups frozen corn kernels, steamed
- 1 (15.5-ounce) can pinto beans, drained and rinsed
- 1 jarred roasted red bell pepper, drained and chopped
- 1 carrot, shredded
- 2 scallions, minced
- 2 tablespoons olive oil
- 1 1/2 tablespoons lime juice or lemon juice
- 1/4 teaspoon ground cumin
- 1/2 teaspoon salt
- 1/8 teaspoon cayenne

In a large bowl, combine the corn, pinto beans, bell pepper, carrot, and scallions.

Drizzle on the olive oil, lime juice, cumin, salt, and cayenne and toss well to combine. Taste and adjust the seasonings, if needed.

MAKES 4 SERVINGS

Southwest Salmagundi

This salad is inspired by those seven-layer dips that sometimes make an appearance around Super Bowl time. Spicy food lovers may want to use hot salsa rather than mild. The asbestos-tongued may go a step further and substitute canned sliced jalapeños for the mild green chiles.

1 (15.5-ounce) can pinto beans, drained
1 (4-ounce) can chopped mild or hot green chiles, drained
2 tablespoons chopped fresh cilantro or parsley
1 tablespoon olive oil
1 tablespoon lime juice or lemon juice
1/2 teaspoon chili powder
1/4 teaspoon ground cumin
1/4 teaspoon garlic powder
Salt
1 (16-ounce) can vegetarian refried beans, heated
1 ripe Hass avocado, pitted, peeled, and diced (optional)
One (12-ounce) jar mild or hot salsa
Tortilla chips, as desired

In a large bowl, combine the pinto beans, chiles, cilantro, olive oil, lime juice, chili powder, cumin, garlic powder, and salt to taste. Stir gently to combine.

Spread the heated refried beans in the center of a large shallow serving bowl or platter or individual shallow bowls. Mound the pinto bean salad on top and top with avocado, if using. Arrange a border of salsa around the outside perimeter of the salad. Surround with tortilla chips.

MAKES 4 SERVINGS

Three's-a-Crowd Bean Salad

Create your own version of three-bean salad – this variation can feature two beans instead of three, but if you're fond of the classics, go ahead and add the optional steamed (fresh or frozen) cut green and/or waxed beans to the mix, as shown opposite.

1 (15.5-ounce) can chickpeas, drained
1 (15.5-ounce) can kidney beans, drained
1 (2-ounce) jar chopped pimentos, drained
1 cup cooked fresh or frozen cut green beans (optional)
1 cup cooked fresh or frozen cut wax beans (optional)
1 tablespoon minced onion or scallions
3 tablespoons olive oil
2 tablespoons white wine vinegar
1 teaspoon sugar
1/2 teaspoon salt
1/8 teaspoon cayenne

In a large bowl, combine the chickpeas, kidney beans, green and/or wax beans (if using), pimentos, and onion. Add the oil, vinegar, sugar, salt, and cayenne. Toss to mix well. Taste and adjust the seasonings, if needed. Set aside for 15 minutes before serving to allow the flavors to meld.

MAKES 4 SERVINGS

White Bean Niçoise Salad

A Niçoise salad makes a flavorful and colorful main-dish salad even using pantry ingredients. Whenever I roast small potatoes, I always make extra with this salad in mind.

  2 cups fresh or frozen cut green beans, steamed and cooled
  2 cups diced cooked potatoes (steamed or roasted)
  1 cup cherry tomatoes, halved or 1 (14-ounce) can diced tomatoes, well drained
  1 (15-ounce) can cannellini beans, drained and rinsed
  1/4 cup pitted Kalamata olives, halved
  3 tablespoons olive oil
  1 1/2 tablespoon white balsamic vinegar
  1 teaspoon Dijon mustard
  1 teaspoon dried basil
  1/4 teaspoon salt
  1/4 teaspoon sugar
  1/4 teaspoon ground black pepper
  Shredded lettuce, to serve (optional)

In a large bowl, combine the green beans, potatoes, tomatoes, cannellini beans, and olives.

In a small bowl, whisk together the oil, vinegar, mustard, basil, salt, sugar, and pepper, and add to the ingredients in the large bowl. Toss gently to combine. Taste to adjust seasonings. Serve on a bed of lettuce, if using.

MAKES 4 SERVINGS

Asian Noodle Salad with Peanut Dressing

This tangle of noodles with a peanut dressing upgrade tastes great. If you like more heat, add another 1/4 teaspoon of red pepper flakes. If you don't like heat, leave it out.

1/2 cup peanut butter
3 tablespoons tamari or other soy sauce
2 tablespoons rice wine vinegar
1/2 teaspoon light brown sugar
1/4 teaspoon red pepper flakes, or to taste
1/8 teaspoon garlic powder
1/2 cup water
8 ounces rice vermicelli or ramen noodles
1 tablespoon toasted sesame oil
1 large carrot, shredded
2/3 cup frozen green peas, thawed
1 (8-ounce) can water chestnuts, drained
1/4 cup dry-roasted peanuts

In a bowl, combine the peanut butter, tamari, vinegar, red pepper flakes, and garlic powder, stirring to blend well. Add the water, stirring until smooth. Set aside.

Soak the noodles in enough boiling water to cover until softened. Drain and transfer to a large bowl. Toss with sesame oil to coat.

Add the carrots, peas, water chestnuts, and peanuts to the bowl with the noodles. Add the reserved peanut sauce, tossing gently to combine.

MAKES 4 SERVINGS

Suddenly Sushi Salad

This salad is an interpretation of chirashi zushi, *or "scattered sushi." It's a great way to enjoy the same delicious flavor of sushi but without all the fuss. For added protein, top with thin strips of baked marinated tofu.*

- 3 cups cooked sushi rice or brown rice, at room temperature
- 2 teaspoons rice vinegar
- 1 teaspoon agave nectar
- 1/2 teaspoon salt
- 1 (12-ounce) jar hearts of palm, drained
- 1 carrot, shredded
- 1 English cucumber, peeled and cut into matchsticks
- 2 scallions, minced
- 1 tablespoon tamari soy sauce
- 1 teaspoon toasted sesame oil
- 1 Hass avocado, pitted, peeled, and cut into 1/2-inch dice (optional)
- 1 (7 by 8-inch) sheet dried nori, cut into 1/4-inch squares or torn into small pieces
- 1 tablespoon toasted sesame seeds or black sesame seeds
- Wasabi paste and pickled ginger, for serving

Place the cooked rice in a large bowl. Add the vinegar, agave, and salt and toss gently to combine. Set aside.

Pulse the hearts of palm in a food processor just enough to shred into bite-size pieces. Transfer to a separate bowl. Add the carrot, cucumber, scallions, tamari, and sesame oil, and toss to coat.

Divide the rice among individual serving bowls. Top each portion with the vegetable mixture, dividing evenly. Top each with the avocado, if using. Scatter the nori and sesame seeds on top of each bowl. Serve with wasabi and pickled ginger.

MAKES 4 SERVINGS

soy sauce, pickled ginger, and rice

soba noodles

Sesame Soba Salad

This hearty main-dish salad is loaded with flavor and is quick and easy to make. A bag of shredded cabbage makes short work of the prep.

8 ounces soba noodles
1 tablespoon toasted sesame oil
2 tablespoons soy sauce
2 tablespoons hoisin sauce
2 tablespoons rice wine vinegar
1 teaspoon sriracha sauce
1 teaspoon grated fresh ginger
1 teaspoon sugar
1 (12-ounce) bag shredded cabbage
1 large carrot, shredded
1/2 cup fresh cilantro leaves
2 scallions, minced
8 ounces seitan or baked tofu, diced or cut into strips

Cook the soba in a pot of boiling water according to package directions. Drain and transfer to a large bowl. Add the sesame oil and toss to coat. Set aside.

In a small bowl, combine the soy sauce, hoisin, vinegar, sriracha, ginger, and sugar, stirring well to blend. Set aside.

Add the shredded cabbage to the bowl with the soba. Add the carrot, cilantro, scallions, and seitan. Pour on the reserved dressing and toss well to combine.

MAKES 4 SERVINGS

Zucchini "Pasta" Salad

Spiralized vegetables, especially zucchini, make a popular alternative to pasta. I especially like it in this "pasta" salad with a creamy avocado dressing. Add more fresh veggies if you have them on hand.

2 medium green zucchini, cut with a spiral slicer
1 cup thinly sliced cucumber
1 carrot, shredded
1 roasted or fresh red bell pepper, chopped
2 scallions, minced
1/4 cup chopped oil-packed or reconstituted sun-dried tomatoes or 1/3 cup cherry
    tomatoes, halved
1/4 cup pitted kalamata olives
1/4 cup chopped fresh basil
1 ripe Hass avocado, pitted and peeled
1 garlic clove, pressed
1/4 cup olive oil
1/4 cup lemon juice, fresh squeezed
1/2 teaspoon salt
1/4 teaspoon ground black pepper
1/4 cup toasted walnut pieces

Place the spiralized zucchini in large bowl. Add the cucumber, carrot, red bell pepper, scallions, tomatoes, olives, and basil. Toss gently to combine.

In a blender, combine the avocado, garlic, olive oil, lemon juice, salt, and pepper. Blend until very smooth and creamy.

Pour the dressing over the salad, add the walnuts, and toss to coat.

MAKES 4 SERVINGS

Asian Noodle Slaw

Why make the same old coleslaw when you can make an Asian noodle slaw? This can be made in just minutes using a bag of shredded cabbage and some ramen (Although you can instead make it with any kind of noodles and shred your own cabbage, if you prefer). Add some diced baked tofu or seitan strips for a hearty one-dish meal.

- 2 ramen noodle bricks, broken into thirds
- 1 (12-ounce) bag shredded cabbage
- 1 carrot, shredded
- 2 scallions, minced
- 2 tablespoons chopped fresh cilantro or parsley
- 2 teaspoons grated fresh ginger
- 3 tablespoons rice vinegar
- 1 1/2 tablespoons safflower oil
- 1 1/2 tablespoons soy sauce
- 2 teaspoons toasted sesame oil
- 1/2 teaspoon sugar
- Salt
- 3 tablespoons chopped peanuts

Cook the noodles in a pot of boiling water until tender. Drain and run under cold water, then transfer to a large bowl. Add the shredded cabbage, carrot, scallions, cilantro, and ginger. Set aside.

In a small bowl, combine the vinegar, safflower oil, soy sauce, sesame oil, sugar, and salt to taste. Stir until well blended.

Pour the dressing over the noodles and vegetables and toss gently to coat. Taste and adjust the seasoning if needed. Sprinkle the peanuts on top. Serve at once or cover and refrigerate until needed.

MAKES 4 SERVINGS

Avocado Goddess Potato Salad

This is the most decadent potato salad I've ever had and one of the most delicious too, thanks to the addition of sun-dried tomatoes, Kalamata olives, and cannellini beans, all cloaked with a creamy goddess dressing made with avocado. Roasting the potatoes adds extra flavor – and cutting them into smaller pieces shortens the roasting time, but if you don't have time, you can steam them or "bake" them in a microwavem or plan ahead and roast them in advance. This salad is best if eaten on the same day that it is made.

1 pound small new potatoes, cut into 1/2-inch pieces
Salt and ground black pepper
1 ripe Hass avocado, peeled and pitted
1 or 2 scallions, chopped
1 or 2 garlic cloves, crushed
3 tablespoons chopped fresh parsley
1/2 cup plain unsweetened almond milk
2 tablespoons rice vinegar
1 tablespoon tahini
1 tablespoon fresh lemon juice
1 tablespoon tamari soy sauce
1 celery rib, finely chopped
1 (15-ounce) can cannellini beans, drained and rinsed
1/3 cup chopped oil-packed or reconstituted sun-dried tomatoes
1/3 cup kalamata olives, pitted and halved
Torn butter lettuce leaves, to serve (optional)

Preheat the oven to 425°F. Arrange the potatoes on a lightly oiled baking pan and spray with a little cooking spray. Season to taste with salt and pepper and roast until just softened and lightly browned, turning once, 15 to 18 minutes. When the potatoes are done, transfer them to a large bowl and set aside to cool.

While the potatoes are roasting, in a blender or food processor, combine the avocado, scallions, garlic, and parsley and process until smooth. Add the almond milk, vinegar, tahini, lemon juice, tamari, and salt and pepper, to taste. Process until creamy. Set aside.

When the potatoes are cool, add the celery, beans, tomatoes, olives, and reserved dressing. Toss to coat. Serve as is or over lettuce.

MAKES 4 SERVINGS

Three-Tomato Pasta Salad

Fresh, canned, and sun-dried tomatoes bring their unique qualities to this delicious pasta salad. For extra protein, add your favorite canned or cooked beans or diced seitan or baked tofu.

8 ounces rotini or other bite-sized pasta
3 tablespoons olive oil
2 garlic cloves, crushed
2 tablespoons rice vinegar
1/2 teaspoon dried basil
1/2 teaspoon dried oregano
1/2 teaspoon sugar
1/4 teaspoon red pepper flakes
Salt and black pepper
1 1/2 cups cherry or grape tomatoes, halved lengthwise
1 (14.5-ounce) can petite diced tomatoes, drained
1/3 cup chopped oil-packed or reconstituted sun-dried tomatoes
1 (6-ounce) jar marinated artichoke hearts, drained
1 celery rib, chopped
1 cup frozen green peas, thawed
1/4 cup fresh basil or parsley (optional)

Cook the pasta in a pot of boiling salted water until just tender, 8 to 10 minutes. Drain and rinse under cold water, then transfer to a large bowl. Set aside.

In a small blender or food processor combine the olive oil, garlic, vinegar, basil, oregano, sugar, red pepper flakes, and salt and pepper to taste. Process to blend.

Pour the dressing over the pasta. Add the three kinds of tomatoes, artichoke hearts, celery, peas, and fresh basil, if using. Toss gently to mix well. Taste and adjust the seasonings, if needed.

MAKES 4 SERVINGS

4

Pizza
Burgers
Sandwiches

Artichoke Muffaleta Po' Boys

The best of two popular New Orleans culinary icons join forces to create the ultimate sandwich in this po'boy made with artichokes and a piquant olive relish.

3 scallions, chopped
1 garlic clove, crushed
1/3 cup pickled vegetables, well-drained
1/3 cup pimiento-stuffed green olives, well-drained
1 tablespoon olive oil
1 (14-ounce) can artichoke hearts, well-drained and halved
1/2 teaspoon Cajun spice blend
3 tablespoons Creole mustard
3 tablespoons vegan mayonnaise
2 small sub rolls, lightly toasted
1 cup shredded lettuce
1 large tomato, thinly sliced
Pickled sliced jalapeños
Tabasco or other hot sauce, to serve

In a food processor, combine the scallion and garlic and process until finely minced. Add the pickled vegetables, olives, and pulse to make a relish. Set aside.

Heat the oil in a large skillet over medium heat. Add the artichoke hearts, season with the spice blend, and cook until nicely browned, about 5 minutes per side.

To assemble the sandwiches, spread the mayonnaise and mustard on the inside top and bottom of the bread. Spread the lettuce onto the bottom of each sandwich, followed by tomato slices. Top with the relish mixture, a few slices of jalapeños, and the artichokes. Serve at once with Tabasco.

MAKES 2 SERVINGS

Homestyle Hash Burgers

These burgers are a tasty way to enjoy your favorite hash. I usually make hash with left-over roasted potatoes and onions mixed with some chopped leftover seitan or vegan meatloaf. This recipe features on-hand pantry ingredients for those times when you're craving the flavor of hash and don't have the leftovers on hand. Instead of serving on rolls, you can serve these on a plate slathered in ketchup.

1 (15.5-ounce) can lentils or kidney beans, rinsed and well drained
1 1/2 cups frozen Tater Tots, thawed
1/2 teaspoon onion powder
1/4 teaspoon ground black pepper
1 (6-ounce) jar roasted red bell peppers, chopped and blotted
1/2 cup frozen green peas, thawed and blotted
1 tablespoon olive oil
4 burger rolls, lightly toasted
To serve: lettuce, pickle chips, ketchup

Mash the beans in a bowl to break them up. Add the Tater Tots, onion powder, and black pepper, and mash to incorporate. Stir in the roasted red bell pepper and green peas and mix well. Divide the mixture into four equal balls and shape into patties.

Heat the oil in large skillet over medium-high heat. Cook until hot and nicely browned on both sides, about 10 minutes total. Serve on toasted rolls with lettuce, pickle chips, and lots of ketchup.

MAKES 4 SERVINGS

Black Bean and Walnut Burgers

These burgers are especially good served on ciabatta rolls with sautéed onions and mushrooms.

2 cloves garlic, crushed
1/2 cup walnut pieces
1/4 cup chopped onion
1 (15-ounce) can black beans, rinsed and drained
1/2 cup old-fashioned oats
1/2 cup vital wheat gluten
1 tablespoon almond butter or tahini
1 tablespoon tamari
Water, as needed
1 teaspoon dried parsley
1/2 teaspoon salt
1/4 teaspoon ground black pepper
Safflower oil
4 burger rolls, toasted
Condiments of choice

In a food processor, combine the garlic, walnuts, and onion, and pulse until finely minced. Add the beans, oats, wheat gluten, almond butter, tamari, parsley, salt, and pepper. Process until well combined. Do not overmix. If the mixture is too dry to hold together, add a small amount of water, 1 tablespoon at a time. Shape the mixture into four equal-sized patties.

Heat a thin layer of oil in a large skillet over medium-high heat. Add the burgers and cook until nicely browned on both sides, 4 to 5 minutes per side. Serve on burger rolls with your favorite condiments

MAKES 4 SERVINGS

Bean and Spinach Burritos

These burritos taste great and couldn't be easier to make with a handful of pantry ingredients.

  1 (15-ounce) can pinto beans, drained
  2 teaspoons chili powder
  10-ounces frozen chopped spinach, thawed and squeezed dry
  1 cup tomato salsa
  1 (4-ounce) can chopped mild green chiles, drained
  4 large flour tortillas
  ½ cup shredded vegan cheese (optional)

Combine the beans and chili powder in a saucepan and mash the beans well. Add the spinach, salsa, and chiles and stir to combine. Cook over medium heat until hot, 6 to 7 minutes, adding a little water if the mixture begins to stick to the pan.

To serve, divide the bean mixture among the tortillas, sprinkle with cheese, if using, and roll up. Serve hot.

MAKES 4 SERVINGS

Crab-Free Sandwiches

Zesty seasonings have a transformative effect on a can of chickpeas in these flavorful crisply fried cakes. They're reminiscent of crab cakes, but in a good way. If you don't want to eat them in a sandwich, serve on plate with a dab of sriracha mayo.

1 (15-ounce) can chickpeas, drained and mashed
1/4 cup vital wheat gluten
3 tablespoons nutritional yeast
1 teaspoon kelp, dulse, or nori powder (optional)
1 tablespoon lemon juice
1 teaspoon Old Bay Seasoning
1/2 teaspoon garlic powder
1/2 teaspoon onion powder
1/2 teaspoon dry mustard
1/4 teaspoon cayenne
Salt and ground black pepper
1/2 cup dried bread crumbs
Olive oil, for frying
Toasted sandwich rolls
Lettuce leaves
Sliced tomato
Vegan mayo
Tabasco sauce

Place the chickpeas in a medium bowl and mash well. Add the vital wheat gluten, nutritional yeast, kelp powder (if using), lemon juice, Old Bay seasoning, garlic powder, onion powder, mustard, cayenne, and salt and pepper to taste. Mix until well combined. Pour the bread crumbs into a shallow bowl. Shape the chickpea mixture into 4 tight patties and dredge in the bread crumbs.

Heat the oil in a large skillet over medium heat. Add the patties and cook until browned on both sides, turning once, about 4 minutes per side. Serve hot on rolls with lettuce tomato, mayo, and Tabasco.

MAKES 4 SERVINGS

BBQ Jack Sandwiches

Look for canned water-packed jackfruit in Asian markets or well-stocked supermarkets (do not to get the kind packed in syrup). If jackfruit is unavailable, substitute your choice of chopped seitan, steamed crumbled tempeh, chopped mushrooms, or reconstituted TVP or Soy Curls.

- 1 tablespoon olive oil
- 1 (16-ounce) can water-packed jackfruit, drained and shredded or thinly sliced
- 1 (4-ounce) can chopped mild or hot green chiles, drained
- 1 cup barbecue sauce
- 1 tablespoon tamari
- 2 teaspoons prepared yellow mustard
- 1/2 teaspoon smoked paprika
- 1/2 teaspoon liquid smoke
- 1/2 teaspoon onion powder
- Salt and ground black pepper
- 4 sandwich rolls, split and toasted

Heat the oil in a saucepan over medium heat. Add the jackfruit and chiles and cook, stirring, for 3 minutes. Stir in the barbecue sauce, tamari, mustard, paprika, liquid smoke, onion powder, and salt and pepper to taste. Cook, stirring occasionally, to heat through and blend the flavors, about 8 minutes. Mix well, adding a little water if the mixture is too dry. Taste and adjust the seasonings, if needed. When ready to serve, spoon the mixture onto the rolls and serve hot.

MAKES 4 SANDWICHES

Artichoke Tartines

Tartine is a classy French word for an open-faced sandwich on toasted bread. The toppings are only limited by your imagination and my imagination especially likes a creamy white bean spread with olives and sun-dried tomatoes and sliced marinated artichokes. This recipe makes enough to serve two people as a meal or four people as an appetizer.

1 cup canned white beans, drained and rinsed
1/3 cup soft sun-dried tomato pieces (rehydrated or oil-packed)
2 tablespoons pitted Kalamata olives
Salt and ground black pepper
1 cup marinated artichoke hearts, drained
4 (1/2-inch thick) slices Italian or sourdough bread

In a food processor, process the white beans until smooth. Add the sun-dried tomatoes and olives. Season with salt and pepper to taste and pulse to combine, leaving some texture. Set aside. Cut the artichoke hearts into slices and set aside.

Toast the bread in an oven, toaster oven, or toaster. Spread each slice of bread with the white bean mixture, then top each with a few slices of artichoke. Serve immediately.

MAKES 2 TO 4 SERVINGS

Texas Caviar Wraps

I first made these wraps when I had some leftover Texas Caviar, a flavorful dip made with black-eyed peas. Now I just bypass the dip and make this as a tasty sandwich filling in the first place.

1 (15-ounce) can black-eyed peas, rinsed and well-drained
1 (14.5-ounce) can diced tomatoes, well-drained
2 teaspoons cider vinegar
1 teaspoon Dijon mustard
1/4 teaspoon garlic powder
1/4 teaspoon onion powder
Splash Tabasco
Salt and ground black pepper
Vegan mayonnaise
3 soft flour tortillas
Shredded lettuce
Pickled jalapeño slices

In a food processor, combine the black-eyed peas, tomatoes, vinegar, mustard, garlic powder, onion powder, Tabasco, and salt and pepper to taste. Pulse until well combined.

Spread a thin layer of vegan mayonnaise on each tortilla. Divide the filling mixture among the tortillas, spreading it in a line in the lower third of each tortilla. Top with shredded lettuce and jalapenos, roll up, and serve.

MAKES 3 SERVINGS

White Bean and Spinach Quesadillas

Frozen spinach and canned white beans combine with garlic and spices to make a delectable filling for these hearty quesadillas. No cheese needed. Serve with your favorite salsa.

1 tablespoon olive oil
3 garlic cloves, pressed or minced
10 ounces frozen spinach, thawed and squeezed dry
Salt and ground black pepper
1 (15.5-ounce) can white beans, drained and rinsed
1 tablespoon lemon juice
1/2 teaspoon ground coriander
1/2 teaspoon ground cumin
2 large flour tortillas

Heat the oil in a saucepan over medium heat. Add the garlic and cook until fragrant, 30 seconds. Add the spinach and season with salt and pepper to taste. Add the beans, lemon juice, coriander, and cumin. Cook, stirring, until the spinach is cooked and the flavors are blended, about 5 minutes. Mash the beans well while cooking. Set aside.

Place two large tortillas on a flat work surface. Divide the spinach mixture evenly between the tortillas. Spread the filling mixture evenly on half of each tortilla. Fold the remaining half of each tortilla over the half with the filling and press gently to enclose and spread the filling close to the edges.

Heat a large nonstick skillet over medium heat. Arrange the quesadillas in the hot skillet, one at a time or both, depending on the size of your skillet. Flatten with a metal spatula and cook until browned on the bottom, about 3 minutes. Flip the quesadillas and cook until the other side is golden brown. Serve hot.

MAKES 2 SERVINGS

Samosadillas

Food cravings can come at the darnedest times, like when you don't feel like cooking. If your samosa craving comes at an inconvenient time, you'll be glad you have a well-stocked pantry to make these samosa-quesadilla hybrids in minutes. Craving satisfied. Note: If you don't have chutney on hand, you can make a tasty facsimile by combining 3 tablespoons of peach jam with 1 to 2 teaspoons of cider vinegar, 1 teaspoon raisins, a pinch of red pepper flakes, and a little grated ginger.

2 cups Tater Tots, thawed
1 cup frozen green peas, thawed
1/4 cup canned hot or mild green chiles, minced
1 scallion, minced or 1 teaspoon dehydrated chives
2 tablespoons raisins
1 tablespoon tamari soy sauce
1 tablespoon curry powder
2 teaspoons ground coriander
1 teaspoon ground cumin
Salt and ground black pepper
2 large flour tortillas
Your favorite chutney (see Note)

Place the Tater Tots in a lightly-oiled skillet over medium heat and mash them with a potato masher or ricer. Add the peas, chiles, scallion, raisins, tamari, curry powder, coriander, cumin, and salt and pepper to taste. Mix well and cook, stirring, until hot, about 5 minutes. Taste and adjust the seasonings, if needed.

Place two large tortillas on a flat work surface. Divide the potato mixture evenly between the tortillas. Spread the filling mixture evenly on half of each tortilla. Fold the remaining half of each tortilla over the half with the filling and press gently to enclose and spread the filling close to the edges.

Heat a large nonstick skillet over medium heat. Arrange the samosadillas in the hot skillet, one at a time or both, depending on the size of your skillet. Flatten with a metal spatula and cook until browned on the bottom, about 3 minutes. Flip the samosadillas and cook until the other side is golden brown. Transfer to a flat work surface and cut into triangles. Serve hot with chutney.

MAKES 2 TO 3 SERVINGS

Chunky Chickpea Sandwiches

This is my go-to sandwich filling. It reminds me of tuna salad but without the fishiness. If you want to add a "taste of the sea" sprinkle in some nori or dulse flakes or kelp powder.

1 (15-ounce) can chickpeas, rinsed and well drained
1/3 cup chopped celery
2 tablespoons minced red onion
1/3 cup vegan mayonnaise
1 teaspoon Dijon mustard
1/2 teaspoon garlic powder
1/8 teaspoon smoked paprika
Salt and ground black pepper
4 slices sandwich bread
2 lettuce leaves, optional
4 tomato slices, optional

Coarsely mash the chickpeas in a bowl. Add the celery, onion, mayonnaise, mustard, garlic powder, paprika, and salt and pepper to taste. Mix well to combine.

Spread the mixture onto two bread slices, top with lettuce and tomato slices, if using, then top with the remaining two slices of bread, cut each sandwich in half, and serve.

MAKES 2 SANDWICHES

Pizza Niçoise

If you keep a few pizza dough balls on hand (I like Trader Joe's brand), a fresh homemade pizza is only minutes away. I keep a few in the freezer and one in the fridge. Be sure to plan ahead so you can bring the dough to room temperature before using.

1 pizza dough, storebought (I like Trader Joe's brand) or homemade (opposite), at room temperature
1/2 cup tomato sauce
1/2 teaspoon dried oregano
1 cup cooked white beans or crumbled tofu
2 garlic cloves, crushed
2 tablespoons nutritional yeast
2 tablespoon reconstituted or oil-packed sun-dried tomatoes, chopped
1/2 teaspoon salt
1/4 teaspoon ground black pepper
1 teaspoon dried basil
1/4 teaspoon red pepper flakes
2 plum tomatoes, cut into thin slices
3 tablespoons chopped pitted kalamata olives
1/2 cup crushed pine nuts

Place the oven rack in the bottom position of the oven. Preheat oven to 450°F.

Stretch the dough onto a lightly oiled pizza pan or baking sheet.

Spread the tomato sauce evenly on top of the pizza dough, to within 1/2-inch of the edge. Sprinkle with the oregano and set aside.

In a food processor, combine the white beans or tofu, garlic, nutritional yeast, sun-dried tomatoes, salt, pepper, dried basil, and red pepper flakes. Process until smooth. Spoon the mixture on top of the tomato sauce and spread a little with the back of a spoon. Arrange the plum tomato slices on top of the pizza and sprinkle with the olives and pine nuts.

Bake until the crust is golden brown, about 15 minutes. Serve hot.

MAKES 1 (12-INCH) PIZZA

Pizza Dough

You can buy ready-made pizza dough (I like Trader Joe's brand) or you can make it yourself with this easy recipe. (Hint: make a few and store them in the freezer.)

3 cups unbleached all-purpose flour
2 1/4 teaspoons instant-rise yeast
1 1/4 teaspoons salt
1/2 teaspoon sugar
1 1/2 tablespoons olive oil
1 cup warm water

Lightly oil the inside of a large bowl and set aside. In a food processor, combine the flour, yeast, salt, and sugar. With the machine running, add the oil through the feed tube and slowly add the water as needed until it forms a slightly sticky dough ball.

Transfer the dough to a floured surface and knead until smooth and elastic, 1 to 2 minutes. Shape the dough into a smooth ball and place it in the prepared bowl. Turn the dough to coat it with oil, cover with plastic wrap and let the dough rise at room temperature in a warm area until doubled in size, about 1 hour.

Punch down the dough and divide it into 2 pieces. On a lightly floured surface, shape each piece into a ball. Cover and let it rest for about 30 minutes. The dough is now ready to use in recipes.

MAKES DOUGH FOR 2 (12-INCH) PIZZAS

Artichoke Pizza with Spinach Pesto

If you make your toppings ahead of time and have your dough at room temperature, this pizza can be assembled and baked in just minutes.

1 pizza dough, storebought (I like Trader Joe's brand) or homemade (page 79), at room
    temperature
1 1/2 cups cooked or 1 (15.5-ounce) can white beans, drained and rinsed
5 garlic cloves, crushed, divided
2 tablespoons water
2 tablespoons lemon juice
3 tablespoons nutritional yeast
1/2 teaspoon dried basil
1/2 teaspoon dried oregano
Salt and ground black pepper
4 cups coarsely chopped spinach
1/2 cup fresh basil leaves
1/3 cup almonds or walnuts
1 (6-ounce) jar marinated artichoke hearts, well drained

Place the oven rack in the bottom position of the oven. Preheat the oven to 450°F. Stretch the dough onto a pizza pan or baking sheet. Bake the crust for 10 minutes, then remove from the oven.

In a food processor, combine the white beans and 2 of the garlic cloves and process to a paste. Add the water, lemon juice, nutritional yeast, basil, and oregano, and salt and pepper to taste. Blend until smooth. Spread the mixture evenly on top of the partially-baked pizza crust, dough, to within 1/2-inch of the edge, and set aside.

In the same food processor, combine the spinach, basil, 3 remaining garlic cloves, and almonds and process to a paste. Add 1/2 teaspoon of salt, and process until smooth. The pesto should be thick. Drop the pesto, by the spoonful, onto the white bean topping, spreading the pesto out slightly so it's not too thick in any one place. Arrange the artichoke hearts on top of the pizza, on top of and in between the pesto. Bake the pizza for an additional 4 to 5 minutes, or until the pizza is hot and the crust is nicely browned. Serve hot.

MAKES 1 (12-INCH) PIZZA

Jalapeño-Hummus Pizza

To save time, use a prepared hummus and a storebought pizza dough.

- 1 pizza dough, storebought (I like Trader Joe's brand) or homemade (page 79), at room temperature
- 1 (15.5-ounce) can chickpeas, drained and rinsed
- 3 garlic cloves, crushed, divided
- 3 tablespoons tahini
- 2 tablespoons lemon juice
- 1/2 teaspoon dried oregano
- Salt and ground black pepper
- 1/4 to 1/3 cup jarred jalapeño slices, well drained

Place the oven rack in the bottom position of the oven. Preheat the oven to 450°F. Stretch the dough onto a pizza pan or baking sheet. Bake the crust for 10 minutes, then remove from the oven.

In a food processor, combine the chickpeas and garlic cloves and process to a paste. Add the tahini, lemon juice, oregano, and salt and pepper to taste. Blend until smooth.

Spread the mixture evenly on top of the partially baked pizza crust, dough, to within 1/2-inch of the edge, and set aside. Arrange the jalapeño slices on top of the hummus.

Bake the pizza for an additional 4 to 5 minutes, or until the pizza is hot and the crust is nicely browned. Serve hot.

MAKES 1 (12-INCH) PIZZA

Black and White Pizza

A layer of garlicky white bean purée topped with black olive tapenade makes this black and white pizza anything but boring. If you don't have a jar of tapenade on hand, you can substitute finely chopped pitted Kalamata olives

1 pizza dough, storebought (I like Trader Joe's brand) or homemade (page 79), at room temperature
1 (15.5-ounce) can white beans, drained and rinsed
3 garlic cloves, crushed
3 tablespoons nutritional yeast
2 tablespoons lemon juice
2 tablespoons water
1/2 teaspoon dried oregano
Salt and ground black pepper
1 (6-ounce) jar black olive tapenade

Place the oven rack in the bottom position of the oven. Preheat the oven to 450°F. Stretch the dough onto a pizza pan or baking sheet. Bake the crust for 10 minutes, then remove from the oven.

In a food processor, combine the white beans and garlic and process to a paste. Add the nutritional yeast, lemon juice, water, oregano, and salt and pepper to taste. Blend until smooth. Spread the mixture evenly on top of the partially-baked pizza crust, dough, to within 1/2-inch of the edge, and set aside.

Drop the tapenade, by the spoonful, onto the white bean topping, spreading the tapenade slightly so it's not too thick in any one place. (You may not need to use all of the tapenade.) Bake the pizza for an additional 4 to 5 minutes, or until the pizza is hot and the crust is nicely browned. Serve hot.

MAKES 1 (12-INCH) PIZZA

BBQ Chickpea Pizza

Just about anything is better with barbecue sauce and pizza is no exception. Instead of or in addition to chickpeas, add some chopped seitan or roasted cauliflower to the topping. If you prefer a saucier topping, add a little extra barbecue sauce when heating the chickpeas.

- 1 pizza dough, store-bought (I like Trader Joe's brand) or homemade (page 79), at room temperature
- 2 (15.5-ounce) cans chickpeas, drained and rinsed
- 1 (4-ounce) can chopped mild or hot green chiles, drained
- 1 cup barbecue sauce, or more if needed
- 1 tablespoon tamari
- 2 teaspoons prepared yellow mustard

Place the oven rack in the bottom position of the oven. Preheat the oven to 450°F. Stretch the dough onto a pizza pan or baking sheet. Bake the crust for 10 minutes, then remove from the oven.

In a saucepan, combine the chickpeas, chiles, barbecue sauce, tamari, and mustard and cook over medium heat for 5 minutes, coarsely mashing the chickpeas against the side of the saucepan.

Spread the mixture evenly on top of the partially-baked pizza crust, dough, to within 1/2-inch of the edge.

Bake the pizza for an additional 4 to 5 minutes, or until the pizza is hot and the crust is nicely browned. Serve hot.

MAKES 1 (12-INCH) PIZZA

Cheeseburger Pizza

Plan ahead so you can soak the cashews and bring your dough to room temperature. For an even quicker pizza, use vegan cheese shreds (such as Daiya) instead of making your own sauce and replace the TVP mixture with fresh ot frozen vegan burger crumbles or chopped veggie burgers.

- 1 pizza dough, store-bought (I like Trader Joe's brand) or homemade (page 79), at room temperature
- 1/2 cup cashews, soaked for 4 hours, then drained
- 1/2 cup almond milk
- 3 tablespoons nutritional yeast
- 2 tablespoons jarred pimientos or roasted red pepper
- 1 tablespoon light miso
- 1 tablespoon tamari
- 2 teaspoons lemon juice
- 1/2 teaspoon Dijon mustard
- 1/2 teaspoon paprika
- Salt and ground black pepper
- 1 tablespoon olive oil
- 1 cup TVP or Soy Curls, reconstituted in hot water for 10 minutes
- 1/2 teaspoon onion powder
- 1 tablespoon ketchup, plus more to serve

Place the oven rack in the bottom position of the oven. Preheat the oven to 450°F. Stretch the dough onto a pizza pan or baking sheet. Bake the crust for 10 minutes, then remove from the oven.

In a blender, combine the drained cashews, almond milk, nutritional yeast, pimientos, miso, tamari, lemon juice, mustard, paprika, and salt and pepper to taste, and blend until smooth. The sauce should be thick. Taste and adjust the seasonings, if needed. Set aside.

Heat the oil in a skillet over medium heat. Drain the TVP well. If using Soy Curls, chop them finely. Add them to the hot skillet and season with onion powder and salt and pepper to taste. Add the ketchup and mix well. Remove from the heat. Spread the cheese sauce evenly on top of the partially-baked pizza crust to within 1/2-inch of the edge. Sprinkle the burger mixture on top. Bake the pizza for an additional 4 to 5 minutes, or until it is hot and the crust is browned. Serve drizzled with extra ketchup, if desired.

MAKES 1 (12-INCH) PIZZA

5

Stovetop Suppers

Cheesy Grits and Greens with Smoky Mushrooms 88
Southwest Polenta 90
Hoppin' John and Collards 91
Paella from the Pantry 92
Asian-Style Vegetable Pancakes 94
Dinnertime Scramble 95
Greek Freekeh and Spinach with White Beans 96
Layered Tortilla Skillet 97
Quick Quinoa Pilaf 99
Lemongrass Jasmine Rice with Asparagus 100
Pinto Bean Nacho Pie 101
Chickpea-Artichoke Cakes with Lemon-Thyme Aioli 102
Pantry Bulgur Pilaf 105
Tofu and Broccoli Stir-Fry 106
Tuscan Chickpea Frittata 107
Black Bean Picadillo 108
Red Beans and Quinoa with Chipotle Queso 109
Top-Shelf Couscous Pilaf 110
Jerk Tempeh with Coconut Quinoa 111

Cheesy Grits and Greens
with Smoky Mushrooms

The addition of nutritional yeast and a little vegan butter give grits a cheesy flavor without the cheese. If you like, you may add 1/2 cup of shredded vegan cheddar for more cheesy goodness. The amount of time needed to cook the greens will depend on the type of greens you use and whether they're fresh or frozen.

1 cup quick-cooking grits
2 teaspoons vegan butter (Earth Balance)
2 tablespoons nutritional yeast
Salt and ground black pepper
1 tablespoon olive oil
4 scallions, minced
3 garlic cloves, minced
8 ounces mushrooms (any kind), sliced or chopped
1 teaspoon liquid smoke
1/2 teaspoon smoked paprika
2 cups chopped fresh or frozen greens (thawed and squeezed, if frozen)
1/2 cup vegetable broth

Cook the grits according to package directions. (It should take about 5 minutes for quick-cooking grits.) Stir in the butter, nutritional yeast, and salt and pepper to taste. Keep warm.

While the grits are cooking, heat the oil in large skillet over medium heat. Add the scallions and garlic and cook 1 minute. Add the mushrooms and cook 3 minutes to soften. Sprinkle on the liquid smoke and smoked paprika, tossing to coat. Add the greens and broth, and season with salt and pepper to taste. Cook, stirring, until the greens are tender, 5 to 8 minutes, depending on the greens. Taste and adjust the seasonings, if needed. To serve, top the grits with the greens and mushroom mixture.

MAKES 4 SERVINGS

Southwest Polenta

Polenta makes a nice change from pasta or rice and precooked polenta insures dinner can be on the table in minutes. In the store, look for either instant polenta or shelf-stable vacuum-sealed packages. If you're using an instant polenta mix, prepare the polenta first and then proceed with the recipe.

1 package pre-cooked polenta, cut into 1/2-inch slices
1 to 2 tablespoons olive oil
1 (16-ounce) jar mild or hot tomato salsa
1 (15.5-ounce) can pinto beans, rinsed and drained
1 cup frozen corn kernels, thawed
1 (4-ounce) can chopped mild or hot chiles, drained
1 teaspoon chili powder
1/2 teaspoon onion powder
Salt and ground black pepper
1 ripe avocado, peeled, pitted, and diced (optional)

Pan-fry the polenta slices in the olive oil in a hot skillet until browned on both sides, about 3 minutes per side. Alternatively, brush the polenta slices with the olive oil and grill them on a hot grill or bake them for 10 minutes on a lightly oiled baking sheet in a 350°F oven.

While the polenta is cooking, combine the remaining ingredients (except the avocado) in a saucepan and heat until hot and the flavors are well combined, about 5 minutes. Spoon the salsa mixture over the polenta and serve topped with the avocado, if using.

MAKES 4 SERVINGS

Hoppin' John and Collards

In the South, Hoppin' John and collards are a New Year's Day tradition to bring prosperity and good fortune in the coming year. Usually, fresh collard greens are cooked separately and served alongside the rice and black-eyed peas. This quicker version employs frozen collards cooked right in with the Hoppin' John for a tasty one-dish meal. If you have cooked rice in the freezer, it defrosts quickly in the microwave or in a colander under running water. You can also substitute a quick-cooking grain such as quinoa, if you prefer. Tabasco and/or vegan sour cream make a good dish even better.

1 tablespoon olive oil
1 medium onion, minced
3 garlic cloves, minced
10 ounces frozen chopped collard greens (thawed and squeezed)
3/4 cup water
1 teaspoon dried thyme
Salt and ground black pepper
2 (15.5-ounce) cans black-eyed peas, drained
2 1/2 to 3 cups cooked brown rice
2 tablespoons vegan bacon bits
1/2 to 1 teaspoon liquid smoke
Tabasco
Vegan sour cream, to serve (optional)

Heat the oil in a large saucepan over medium heat. Add the onion, cover, and cook for 5 minutes. Stir in the garlic and thyme and cook for 30 second. Add the collards and water and season with salt and pepper to taste. Cover and cook for 5 minutes longer, then stir in the black-eyed peas, cooked rice, bacon bits, liquid smoke, and a splash of Tabasco. Reduce the heat to low, cover and cook for about 10 minutes or until the flavors have melded, stirring occasionally, adding a little more water if needed to prevent it from sticking. Serve hot with Tabasco and sour cream, if using.

MAKES 4 SERVINGS

Paella from the Pantry

This paella is the ultimate in delicious pantry cooking. The quickest way to get it on the table is by having cooked rice on hand. If you have cooked rice in the freezer, it defrosts quickly in the microwave. You can also substitute a quick-cooking grain such as quinoa, if you prefer.

1 tablespoon olive oil
1 large yellow onion, chopped
3 cloves garlic cloves, minced
1 cup vegetable broth
1 pinch saffron threads or ground turmeric (for color)
1 teaspoon smoked paprika
1 teaspoon dried oregano
1/2 teaspoon red pepper flakes
1 (28-ounce) can diced fire-roasted tomatoes, undrained
Salt and ground black pepper
1 cup frozen green peas, thawed
1 (15.5-ounce) can chickpeas, drained and rinsed
2 1/2 to 3 cups cooked rice
1 (6-ounce) jar marinated artichoke hearts, drained and chopped
1 (6-ounce) jar roasted red bell pepper, drained and chopped
1/2 cup sliced pimiento-stuffed green olives
2 tablespoons chopped fresh parsley

Heat the oil in a large saucepan or Dutch oven over medium heat. Add the onion and cook for 5 minutes to soften. Add the garlic and cook 1 minute longer. Stir in the broth, saffron, paprika, bay leaf, oregano, red pepper flakes, and tomatoes and their juice. Bring to a boil, then lower the heat to medium. Season with salt and pepper to taste, cover, and simmer for 8 minutes. Stir in the peas, chickpeas, cooked rice, artichoke hearts, roasted red bell pepper, olives, and parsley. Cook 3 to 5 minutes longer, stirring gently, to heat through. Taste and adjust the seasonings, if needed. Serve hot.

MAKES 4 SERVINGS

Asian-Style Vegetable Pancakes

These pancakes are easy to make and fun to eat. Best of all, you can use up whatever veggies you have on hand. The two large pancakes are enough to serve two people as a meal, or four to six people as an appetizer.

Dipping Sauce
1/4 cup soy sauce
3 tablespoons rice vinegar
2 tablespoons sake or mirin
2 tablespoons water
1 teaspoon sesame oil
1 teaspoon sugar
1/2 teaspoon hot chili oil or red pepper flakes

Pancakes
1/2 cup all-purpose flour
2 tablespoons tapioca starch
1/2 teaspoon salt
1/4 teaspoon onion powder
1 teaspoon sesame seeds
3/4 cup water
2 cups finely shredded vegetables or chopped leftover cooked vegetables
Safflower oil, for frying

Dipping Sauce: In a small bowl, combine all the sauce ingredients and mix well. Set aside.

Pancakes: In a medium bowl, combine the flour, tapioca starch, salt, onion powder, and sesame seeds. Stir in the water and mix until blended. Add the vegetables and stir to combine.

Heat 1 tablespoon safflower oil in a large nonstick skillet over medium heat. Ladle about one half of the batter into the hot skillet, tilting the pan to form a thin pancake. Cook until firm and nicely browned, about 5 minutes. Flip the pancake to cook the other side for 3 minutes or until browned.

Transfer the pancake to a plate and cover with foil to keep warm while you cook the remaining pancake, adding more oil to the pan, if needed. Cut the pancakes into wedges and serve hot with the dipping sauce on the side.

MAKES 2 LARGE PANCAKES

Dinnertime Scramble

I've always loved "breakfast for dinner" and one of my favorites is a tofu scramble served with toasted bread. You can add whatever ingredients you have on hand, so the variety is almost limitless. Among my favorite additions are sautéed onion and bell pepper, sautéed mushrooms, and chopped vegan bacon. I like to keep frozen onion and pepper strips on hand to use in scrambles and save on prep work. A sprinkle of vegan cheese shreds is also a good addition as are leftover veggies, especially roasted potatoes. Feel free to mix and match add-ins according to your preference and what you have on hand.

1 tablespoon olive oil
1 cup sliced mushrooms (any kind)
3 strips vegan bacon, chopped
1 cup frozen onion and bell pepper strips, thawed and chopped
1 (14-ounce) package firm tofu, drained, patted dry and crumbled
3 tablespoons nutritional yeast flakes
1/8 teaspoon ground turmeric
Salt and ground black pepper
1/3 cup vegan shredded cheese (optional)

Heat the oil in a large nonstick skillet over medium heat. Stir in the mushrooms and vegan bacon and cook for 4 minutes, then stir in the onion and bell pepper and cook for 3 minutes longer. Stir in the tofu, nutritional yeast, turmeric, and salt and pepper to taste. Cook, stirring, for 3 minutes to heat through and combine the ingredients. Stir in the cheese, if using. Taste and adjust the seasoning, if needed. Cook, turning occasionally with a spatula, until the cheese melts, about 2 minutes. Serve hot.

MAKES 4 SERVINGS

Greek Freekeh and Spinach with White Beans

Popular in Northern Africa and the Middle East, freekeh (which means "to rub" in Arabic) is made from roasted wheat, harvested when young, then lightly roasted. The flavor is subtly smoky and it cooks quickly, making it a good choice for speedy meals. In this recipe it combines with spinach, white beans, and Greek seasonings. If you don't have freekeh on hand, you can make this recipe with your favorite grain (allowing for a cooking time difference, depending on what grain you use).

2 1/4 cups water or vegetable broth
1 cup cracked freekeh
1 tablespoon olive oil
Salt
9 ounces fresh baby spinach or frozen chopped spinach, thawed and squeezed
1 (15-ounce) can cannellini beans, rinsed and drained
1 teaspoon dried oregano
Ground black pepper
1/2 cup pitted Kalamata olives, halved lengthwise
1 tablespoon minced fresh dill or 1 teaspoon dried
1 teaspoon lemon juice

Bring the water or vegetable broth to a boil in a saucepan. Add the freekeh, olive oil, and salt to taste. Reduce the heat to a simmer, cover, and cook until tender, 15 to 18 minutes. About 5 minutes before the freekeh is tender, stir in the spinach, white beans, oregano, and black pepper.

Once the freekeh is tender, stir in the olives, dill, and lemon juice. Taste and adjust the seasonings, adding more salt and pepper if needed.

MAKES 4 SERVINGS

Layered Tortilla Skillet

Salsa, chiles, pinto beans, and tortillas team up for a zesty skillet supper. If you have shredded vegan cheddar, sprinkle it on top instead of the nutritional yeast.

1 (15.5-ounce) can pinto beans, rinsed and drained
1 (4-ounce) can chopped green chiles, drained (hot or mild)
1/2 teaspoon chili powder, or more to taste
1/4 teaspoon dried oregano
1 (24-ounce) jar salsa (hot or mild)
Salt and ground black pepper
8 (7-inch) flour tortillas
Nutritional yeast (optional)

In a bowl, combine the pinto beans, chiles, chili powder, and oregano. Stir in half the salsa and mix well. Season with salt and pepper to taste. Mash the pinto mixture with a potato ricer to break up ingredients. Set aside.

Spread half of the remaining salsa in the bottom of a deep skillet. Top with half of the tortillas, overlapping as necessary. Top the tortillas with the reserved bean mixture. Then top with the remaining tortillas. Spread the remaining salsa mixture on top.

Cover with a tight-fitting lid and cook over medium-low heat for 15 minutes to heat through. Sprinkle with nutritional yeast, if using.

MAKES 4 SERVINGS

Quick Quinoa Pilaf

Extremely high in protein and quick-cooking, quinoa is an ideal grain for pantry cooking. It adapts well to various seasonings and is especially delicious when prepared pilaf-style.

3 cups vegetable broth
1 1/2 cups quinoa, well rinsed and drained
1/2 cup minced onion
Salt and ground black pepper
1 carrot, grated
1 cup thawed frozen green peas
2 scallions, minced
1/4 cup toasted slivered almonds
2 tablespoons chopped fresh parsley, cilantro, dill, or basil

Bring the broth to a boil in a saucepan. Add the quinoa and onion. Reduce the heat to low and season to taste with salt and pepper. Cover and cook until the water is nearly absorbed, about 10 minutes. Stir in the carrot, peas, and scallion. Cover again and cook a few minutes longer until the water is absorbed. Remove from the heat, stir in the almonds and parsley. Taste and adjust the seasonings, if needed. Serve hot.

MAKES 4 SERVINGS

Lemongrass Jasmine Rice with Asparagus

Jasmine rice usually takes less than 20 minutes to cook, so it's a great choice when you don't have cooked rice in the fridge or freezer. I love it for its wonderful fragrance that is enhanced further in this dish by the lemongrass and ginger.

1 tablespoon safflower oil
2 garlic cloves, minced
1 tablespoon minced lemongrass
2 teaspoons grated ginger
1/4 teaspoon red pepper flakes
1 cup jasmine rice, well rinsed
1 1/2 cups vegetable broth or water
1 tablespoon white miso
8 ounces fresh or frozen asparagus, cut into 1-inch pieces
Salt
1/2 cup chopped roasted cashews

Heat the oil in a large saucepan over medium high heat. Add the garlic, lemongrass, ginger, and red pepper flakes, and cook until fragrant, 30 seconds. Stir in the rice and broth and bring to a boil. Reduce the heat to a simmer, cover, and cook for 10 minutes, then stir in the miso, asparagus, and salt to taste. Cover and cook until the rice and asparagus are tender and the liquid is absorbed, about 7 minutes. Sprinkle with chopped cashews and serve hot.

MAKES 4 SERVINGS

Pinto Bean Nacho Pie

Everything you love about nachos comes together in this savory pie. The active time is minimal, but be sure to allow extra time for soaking the cashews and chilling the crust.

Crust
1/2 cup raw cashews, soaked in hot water for 1 hour, then drained
1 tablespoon roasted red bell pepper or jarred pimientos, blotted dry
1 garlic clove crushed
1 tablespoon cider vinegar
2 tablespoons nutritional yeast
1/4 teaspoon salt
1/4 teaspoon onion powder
1/4 teaspoon smoked paprika or chili powder
Pinch of ground turmeric (for color)
1/4 cup unrefined coconut oil, melted
2 cups corn chips, crushed

Toppings
1/3 cup vegan sour cream
1/4 teaspoon chili powder or to taste
1 (15-ounce) can pinto beans, drained and rinsed
3/4 cup tomato salsa
1/3 cup bottled sliced jalapeños
1/2 cup chopped pitted Kalamata olives

Crust: In a food processor or high-speed blender, combine the cashews, roasted red bell pepper, garlic, and vinegar. Process until smooth. Add the nutritional yeast, salt, onion powder, paprika, and turmeric. Process until smooth, scraping down the sides as needed. Add the melted coconut oil and process until the mixture is completely smooth, scraping down the sides as needed. Transfer the mixture to a bowl. Stir in the crushed corn chips, mixing well. Press the mixture into a lightly oiled 9-inch pie plate, cake pan, or springform pan. Cover and refrigerate for 2 hours to firm up.

Toppings: While the crust is chilling, prepare the toppings. In a small bowl, combine the sour cream and chili powder. Set aside. In a small saucepan, combine the beans and salsa and cook, stirring, until heated through. Keep warm. When ready to serve, top the crust with the warm beans and salsa mixture, jalapeños, and olives. Drizzle with the re-served sour cream. Cut into wedges and serve.

MAKES 4 TO 6 SERVINGS

Chickpea-Artichoke Cakes with Lemon-Thyme Aioli

The flavor of artichokes and chickpeas pair nicely with the easy thyme aioli in these savory cakes that are equally delicious on a plate or in a toasted bun. You can also shape the cakes into small bites and enjoy them as an appetizer.

1/4 cup old-fashioned oats
3 garlic cloves
1/4 cup coarsely chopped onion or scallions
1/4 cup walnuts pieces
1 (15-ounce) can chickpeas, rinsed, drained, and blotted dry
1 (6-ounce) jar marinated artichoke hearts, drained and blotted dry
2 tablespoons nutritional yeast
2 tablespoons chopped parsley
1 tablespoon fresh lemon juice
1/2 teaspoon dried thyme
1 teaspoon salt
1/4 teaspoon ground black pepper
1/4 cup bread crumbs, or more as needed
2 tablespoons olive oil
Lemon-Thyme Aoli (recipe follows)

In a food processor, process the oats to a flour. Remove from the food processor and set aside. In the same food processor (no need to clean it) process the onion and garlic until finely minced. Add the walnuts, chickpeas, and artichokes and pulse to chop. Add the reserved oat flour, nutritional yeast, parsley, lemon juice, thyme, salt, and pepper. Pulse the mixture until it is finely chopped and well mixed. Transfer the mixture to a bowl. Squeeze some of the mixture in your hand to see if it holds together. If it does not, stir in a little flour or cornstarch. Taste the mixture and adjust the seasonings, if needed. Divide the mixture into 4 equal portions and use your hands to shape into patties. Place the bread crumbs in a shallow bowl and dredge the patties in the bread crumbs. Place the patties on a plate and refrigerate or freeze for 30 minutes to firm up.

Heat oil in a non-stick skillet over medium heat. Place the patties in the pan and cook until golden brown on both sides, turning once, about 10 minutes total.

MAKES 4 SERVINGS

Lemon-Thyme Aioli

1/2 cup vegan mayonnaise
1 tablespoon lemon juice
1 teaspoon fresh or dried thyme, or more
1/2 teaspoon Dijon mustard
Salt and ground black pepper, to taste

Combine all the ingredients in a small bowl and stir until well blended. Refrigerate until needed.

MAKES 1/2 CUP

Pantry Bulgur Pilaf

Also called cracked wheat, bulgur is a quick-cooking grain with a hearty nut-like flavor that is used to make the popular Middle Eastern salad, tabbouleh. It matches perfectly with the sweet/tart cranberries and crunchy almonds. For more color, add a cup of thawed frozen peas when you add the bulgur. If you're not a fan of bulgur, you can make this pilaf using rice, quinoa, or freekeh, if you prefer.

2 cups vegetable broth
1 cup medium bulgur
1 carrot, finely shredded (optional)
2 scallions, minced or 1 tablespoon dehydrated minced onion or chives
Salt and freshly ground black pepper
1/2 cup dried cranberries
1/2 cup toasted slivered almonds
2 tablespoons fresh chopped parsley, cilantro, or mint (optional)

Bring the broth to a boil in a large saucepan. Add the bulgur, carrot (if using), and scallions and stir to combine. Reduce the heat to a simmer and season with salt and pepper to taste. Cover and simmer until the bulgur is tender and the liquid is absorbed, about 10 minutes. Remove the pan from the heat and stir in the cranberries, almonds, and parsley, if using. Cover and let stand for 5 to 7 minutes.

MAKES 4 SERVINGS

Tofu and Broccoli Stir-Fry

The ingredients in this delicious stir-fry can be varied according to what you have on hand. Add sliced fresh mushrooms, substitute bok choy for the broccoli, or use seitan or reconstituted soy curls instead of tofu. Serve over hot cooked rice or toss with leftover cooked noodles if you have some in the fridge.

2 tablespoons safflower oil
14 ounces extra-firm tofu, drained and cut into 1/2-inch dice
3 tablespoons tamari
1 teaspoon grated ginger
3 garlic cloves, minced
1 cup frozen onion and bell pepper strips
2 to 3 cups small broccoli florets (fresh or frozen)
1/4 cup vegetable broth
3 tablespoons mirin
1 (8-ounce) can water chestnuts, rinsed well and drained
1 tablespoon rice vinegar
1 tablespoon toasted sesame seed oil
1 teaspoon sambal oelek or other Asian chili paste
1/4 teaspoon sugar
2 tablespoons chopped roasted peanuts or cashews

Heat 1 tablespoon of the oil in a large skillet over medium-high heat. Add the tofu and stir-fry for 4 minutes or until lightly browned. Splash with 1 tablespoon of the tamari about halfway through. Remove the tofu from the skillet and return the skillet to the heat. Add the remaining safflower oil, then stir in the garlic and ginger and cook until fragrant, 30 seconds. Add the onion and pepper strips, and the broccoli and stir-fry for 1 minutes, then stir in the broth, mirin, and water chestnuts and cook until the vegetables are softened, about 5 minutes. Add the remaining tamari, rice vinegar, sesame oil, sambal oelek, and sugar. Return the tofu to the skillet and stir-fry for a few minutes to heat through. Serve hot sprinkled with the peanuts.

MAKES 4 SERVINGS

Tuscan Chickpea Frittata

Because both the Tuscan pancake known as farinata and the Indian pancake known as pudla are both made with chickpea flour, I was inspired to combine elements of both to make a vegan frittata. This recipe makes one fritatta, but the recipe is easily doubled – it's just better to make the fritattas one at a time since they cook better when spread thinly in the skillet.

- 2/3 cup chickpea flour (besan)
- 1 1/2 tablespoons nutritional yeast
- 1/2 teaspoon baking powder
- 1/2 teaspoon dried basil
- 1/2 teaspoon salt
- 1/4 teaspoon onion powder
- 1/4 teaspoon garlic powder
- 1/8 teaspoon ground turmeric
- 1/8 teaspoon ground black pepper
- 2/3 cup water
- 1 tablespoon lemon juice
- 1/4 cup oil-packed or reconstituted sun-dried tomatoes, chopped
- 1/4 cup pitted kalamata olives, chopped
- 1 cup chopped fresh baby spinach or 1/2 cup frozen chopped spinach, thawed and squeezed dry

In a mixing bowl, combine the chickpea flour, nutritional yeast, baking powder, basil, salt, onion powder, garlic powder, turmeric, and black pepper and mix well. Add the water and lemon juice and stir to mix well, then stir in the tomatoes, olives, and spinach.

Coat a large nonstick skillet with cooking spray and heat over medium heat. Transfer the mixture to the hot skillet and spread evenly with a spatula or the back of a spoon. Cook for 4 minutes, or until the bottom is lightly browned and the edges are dry, then flip it carefully with a spatula. Cook the frittata for an additional 3 minutes on the other side. Serve hot.

MAKES 1 TO 2 SERVINGS

Black Bean Picadillo

Black beans replace ground meat in this flavorful Latin American dish known for tasty inclusions such as raisins and olives. If you don't have cooked rice in the fridge or freezer, you can cook up some quick-cooking brown rice, quinoa, or freekeh while you make the rest of the recipe and it will be ready at the same time. If you don't want to use the wine in this recipe, substitute vegetable broth or water.

1 tablespoon olive oil
1 medium onion, minced
4 garlic cloves, minced
1 teaspoon dried oregano
1 teaspoon ground coriander
1 teaspoon ground cumin
1/2 cup dry red wine
3 tablespoons tomato paste
1 cup vegetable broth
1 (15-ounce) can black beans, rinsed and drained
1 jarred roasted red bell pepper, chopped
1/2 cup pitted green olives, sliced
1/2 cup raisins
2 cups cooked rice
Salt and ground black pepper
1/4 cup chopped cilantro
1/4 cup toasted pumpkin seeds (pepitas)

Heat the oil in a large pot over medium-high heat. Add the onion and cook until softened, 5 minutes. Stir in the garlic and cook until fragrant, 30 seconds. Stir in the oregano, coriander, and cumin, then add the wine and cook, stirring for 2 to 3 minutes, until most of the liquid has evaporated. Add the tomato paste and cook for 30 seconds. Stir in the broth until well blended. Add the black beans, bell pepper, olives, and raisins. Stir in the cooked rice and season with salt and pepper to taste.

Cook, stirring occasionally, to heat through and blend the flavors, about 5 minutes. Serve sprinkled with the cilantro and pumpkin seeds.

MAKES 4 SERVINGS

Red Beans and Quinoa with Chipotle Queso

Plan ahead so you can soak the cashews in water for three hours – if you forget, you can soak them in boiling water for 15 minutes instead. Brown rice or other grains may be used instead of the quinoa, but cooking times will vary.

1 tablespoon olive oil
3 garlic cloves, minced
1 1/2 cups quinoa, well rinsed
1 tablespoon dehydrated minced onion
1/2 teaspoon dried thyme
1/2 teaspoon ground cumin
1/2 teaspoon salt
2 1/4 cups water
1 (15.5-ounce) can dark red kidney beans, drained
1 (4-ounce) can chopped mild green chiles, drained
1/2 cup cashews, soaked for 3 hours, then drained
1/2 cup almond milk
3 tablespoons nutritional yeast
1 chipotle in adobo
1 tablespoon tamari
2 teaspoons lemon juice
1/2 teaspoon smoked paprika
Salt and ground black pepper

Heat the oil in a saucepan over medium heat. Add the garlic and cook until fragrant, 30 seconds. Stir in the quinoa to coat with oil. Add the thyme, cumin, and salt stirring to combine. Stir in the water, cover, and cook until the quinoa is just tender, about 10 minutes. Stir in the beans, chiles, and cook until the quinoa is tender and the water is absorbed, about 5 minutes longer. Taste and adjust seasonings, if needed. Remove from the heat and set aside, covered, to keep warm.

While the quinoa is cooking, make the sauce. In a high-speed blender or food processor, combine the drained cashews with the almond milk and blend until smooth. Add the nutritional yeast, chipotle, tamari, lemon juice, paprika, and salt and pepper to taste. Blend until smooth and creamy. Taste and adjust the seasonings if needed. To serve, spoon the beans and quinoa into a serving bowl or individual bowls and top with the sauce.

MAKES 4 SERVINGS

Top-Shelf Couscous Pilaf

This almost-instant couscous pilaf is tasty, filling, and ready in 10 minutes. If you have fresh quick-cooking veggies on half such as spinach, stir it right in with the couscous and shredded carrot. If you have leftover cooked vegetables you want to add, stir them in when you add the peas.

2 cups water or vegetable broth
1 cup couscous
1 carrot, shredded
1 tablespoon dehydrated minced onion or 2 scallions, minced
1 teaspoon ground coriander
1/2 teaspoon ground cumin
1/4 teaspoon ground cayenne
1 (15.5-ounce) can chickpeas, rinsed and drained
1 cup frozen peas, thawed
1/2 cup chopped pecans or slivered almonds
Salt and ground black pepper
Fresh chopped cilantro, basil, or parsley (optional)

Bring the water to a boil in a saucepan. Stir in the couscous, carrot, onion, coriander, cumin, and cayenne. Cover, turn off the heat and let sit for 10 minutes. Stir in the chickpeas, peas, and pecans. Season to taste with salt and pepper and serve sprinkled with cilantro, if using.

MAKES 4 SERVINGS

Jerk Tempeh with Coconut Quinoa

Coconut quinoa is the perfect foil for the bold flavor of jerk-spiced tempeh. If you have time, simmer the tempeh in water for 15 minutes before using to mellow the flavor and make it more digestible. Serve with a side of sauteed greens.

1 1/2 cups unsweetened coconut milk
1 1/4 cups quinoa, well rinsed
1/4 cup dried shredded coconut
1 teaspoon salt, divided
1 tablespoon safflower oil
8 ounces tempeh, cut into 1/2-inch slices
3 scallions, chopped
2 garlic cloves, minced
2 teaspoons grated fresh ginger
1/4 cup vegetable broth
1 tablespoon tamari soy sauce
2 teaspoons dark brown sugar
1 teaspoon dried thyme
1/2 teaspoon red pepper flakes or cayenne, to taste
1/2 teaspoon ground allspice
1/2 teaspoon ground black pepper
1 tablespoon lime juice

Heat the coconut milk in a saucepan over high heat and bring just to a boil. Stir in the well-rinsed quinoa, dried coconut, and 1/2 teaspoon of the salt. When the coconut milk begins to return to a boil, reduce the heat to low, cover, and cook for 15 minutes, then remove from the heat, cover, and set aside for 5 minutes.

While the quinoa is cooking, heat the oil in a large skillet over medium-high heat. Add the tempeh and cook until browned all over, about 5 minutes. Reduce the heat to medium. Add the scallions, garlic, and ginger and cook 1 minute. Stir in the broth, tamari, sugar, thyme, red pepper flakes, allspice, remaining 1/2 teaspoon salt, and black pepper. Simmer for 5 minutes or longer to blend the flavors. Drizzle with the lime juice. To serve, transfer the quinoa into a large bowl or onto individual plates or shallow bowls and top with the tempeh mixture.

MAKES 4 SERVINGS

6

Pantry Pasta Plus

Giardiniera Mac and Cheese 114
Puttanesca in a Pinch 116
Capellini with Palm-Heart Scampi Sauce 117
Ramen Fagiole 118
Penne and Broccoli with Red Bell Pepper-Walnut Sauce 119
Kitchen-Sink Capellini 120
Artichoke-Cannelini Linguine 122
Penne with White Beans and Olivada 123
Rotini with Creamy Pumpkin Sauce and Walnuts 125
Pasta Marinara 126
Manchurian Black Bean Noodles 127
Speedy Lasagna 128
Noodles with Spicy Peanut Sauce 129
Spaghetti Lo-Mein 130

Giardiniera Mac and Cheese

Italian pickled mixed vegetables, called giardiniera, can be quite tart, so it's best to drain and rinse before using. You can make this mac and cheese without the gardiniera or with the addition of cooked vegetables, frozen, thawed green peas, or marinated artichoke hearts. You can also make this ahead and then cover and pop it in the oven to reheat.

8 ounces fiore pasta or other bite-sized pasta shape
2 1/2 cups giardiniera vegetables, drained and coarsely chopped
1 tablespoon olive oil
1/3 cup panko crumbs
2 cups unsweetened almond milk
1/2 cup raw cashew pieces, soaked and drained
2 tablespoons cornstarch or tapioca starch
1/4 cup nutritional yeast
1 tablespoon mellow white miso
1 heaped tablespoon tomato paste
2 teaspoons apple cider vinegar or lemon juice
3/4 teaspoon mustard powder
1/2 teaspoon smoked paprika
1/2 teaspoon onion powder
1/2 teaspoon garlic powder
1 small clove minced garlic
1/4 teaspoon ground turmeric
1 teaspoon salt, or to taste

Cook the pasta in a pot of boiling salted water until it is al dente. About 3 minutes before the pasta is done cooking, stir in the giardiniera. Drain and leave in the strainer.

Heat the oil in a small skillet over medium-high heat. Add the panko crumbs, stirring to coat with the oil. Cook, stirring for a few minutes until the crumbs are toasted. Remove from the heat and set aside.

In a blender, combine all of the remaining ingredients and blend until smooth and creamy. Pour the sauce into the pot in which the pasta was cooked and cook stirring, over medium-high heat, until the sauce is hot, bubbly, and thickened, about 4 minutes. Add the pasta and vegetables to the sauce, stirring gently to combine and heat through. Transfer to a casserole dish and sprinkle with the reserved panko. Serve hot.

MAKES 4 SERVINGS

Puttanesca in a Pinch

The name of this piquant pasta sauce means "streetwalker style," because ladies of the evening prepare it quickly at the end of a long night's work. It is redolent of garlic, olives, and capers and can have as much heat as you like.

    8 to 12 ounces of your favorite pasta
    Salt
    2 tablespoons olive oil
    5 large garlic cloves, finely chopped
    1 (28-ounce) can crushed tomatoes
    1/2 cup pitted and sliced Kalamata olives
    1/4 cup pitted and sliced green olives
    2 tablespoons capers, drained and chopped
    1/2 teaspoon red pepper flakes, or to taste
    1 teaspoon dried parsley
    1/2 teaspoon dried basil
    1/2 teaspoon dried oregano
    Ground black pepper

Cook the pasta in a pot of boiling salted water until it is just tender. Drain well and return to the pot.

While the pasta is cooking, heat the oil in a saucepan over medium heat. Add the garlic and cook until fragrant, about 1 minute. Stir in the tomatoes, black and green olives, capers, red pepper flakes, and parsley. Season with salt and pepper to taste. Reduce heat to low and simmer for 10 minutes to blend flavors, stirring occasionally. Taste and adjust the seasonings if needed.

To serve, transfer the hot cooked pasta to a large serving bowl or individual shallow bowls and top with the sauce.

MAKES 4 SERVINGS

Capellini with Palm-Heart Scampi Sauce

Chopped hearts of palm stand in for seafood in the garlicky "scampi" sauced pasta dish.

- 8 ounces capellini or angel hair pasta
- Salt
- 2 tablespoons olive oil
- 4 garlic cloves, minced
- 1 (14-ounce) jar hearts of palm, drained and chopped
- 1 tablespoon dulse or nori flakes (optional)
- 1 teaspoon dried oregano
- 1/2 teaspoon dried basil
- 1/2 teaspoon red pepper flakes (optional)
- Ground black pepper
- 1 cup grape or cherry tomatoes, halved lengthwise or 1/3 cup oil-packed or reconstituted sun-dried tomatoes, cut into strips
- 2 tablespoons dry sherry or white wine
- 2 tablespoons fresh lemon juice
- 1/4 cup packed finely chopped parsley

Cook the pasta in a large pot of boiling salted water until it is just tender, about 5 minutes. Drain and return the pasta to the pot. Add 1 tablespoon of the oil and toss to coat. Set aside.

While the pasta is cooking, heat the remaining 1 tablespoon olive oil in a large skillet over medium heat. Add the garlic and cook until fragrant, about 1 minute. Stir in the hearts of palm, dulse (if using), oregano, basil, red pepper flakes (if using), and salt and pepper to taste. Cook, stirring, for 3 minutes to heat through and blend the flavors. Stir in the tomatoes, sherry, lemon juice, and parsley, then taste and adjust the seasonings, if needed. Add the sauce to the cooked pasta and toss to combine and heat through. Serve hot.

MAKES 4 SERVINGS

Ramen Fagiole

East meets West in this tasty use of ramen noodles in the popular Tuscan bean and pasta dish. If you prefer, you can use elbow macaroni or other bite-sized pasta in place of the ramen.

4 ramen noodle bricks
1 (28-ounce) can crushed tomatoes
1 (15.5-ounce) can pinto or cannelini beans, drained
1 teaspoon dried basil
1 teaspoon dried oregano
1/2 teaspoon garlic powder
1/4 teaspoon onion powder
1/4 to 1/2 teaspoon crushed red pepper
Salt and ground black pepper

Break the noodle bricks into small pieces and transfer to a saucepan with enough boiling water to cover. Stir to break up the noodles as they soften.

Add the remaining ingredients. Cook, stirring, over medium heat for 7 to 9 minutes, or until the ingredients are well blended and the mixture is hot. Taste and adjust seasonings, adding a bit more water or seasonings, if needed. Serve hot.

MAKES 4 SERVINGS

Pasta Tips

Most recipes consider 8 ounces of pasta enough for 4 servings, however, sometimes, you might want a little more. Add the fact that different pasta types and brands range in weight from 8 ounces to over a pound, and it may be confusing as to how much pasta to cook. Do what I do: cook the whole box of pasta. That way, even if you only use half of it, you'll have already cooked pasta leftover to make another day with a different sauce. Some of my favorite meals were spontaneously made by combining leftover pasta with other odds and ends in from the refrigerator, freezer, and pantry. Some of the best Asian noodle stir-fries I've had were made with pasta that was leftover from an Italian pasta meal the night before. The sauces or toppings of most of these recipes will comfortably combine with 8 ounces of cooked pasta, but you can stretch the sauce to cover most pasta, depending on how "saucy" you like your pasta dishes. The choice is yours.

Penne and Broccoli with Red Bell Pepper-Walnut Sauce

Pomegranate molasses adds an exotic flavor to the luxurious red pepper walnut sauce, but the dish is still delicious without it if you don't have any on hand. I like this dish with penne but you can use any pasta shape you like. You can also substitute another vegetable for the broccoli (frozen green peas are good here).

8 ounces penne
Salt
3 cups small broccoli florets
2 garlic cloves, minced
1/2 cup walnut pieces
1 (12-ounce) jar roasted red bell peppers, drained
2 tablespoons tomato paste
2 tablespoon olive oil
1 tablespoon pomegranate molasses or agave
2 teaspoons sherry vinegar or lemon juice
1 teaspoon ground cumin
1 teaspoon red pepper flakes
1/2 teaspoon onion powder
1/8 teaspoon allspice
Ground black pepper

Cook the pasta in a large pot of boiling salted water until just tender. About 4 minutes before the pasta is done cooking, add the broccoli. Drain the pasta and broccoli and return to the pot, reserving 1/2 cup of the hot pasta water.

While the pasta is cooking, combine the walnuts and garlic in a food processor and process until finely ground. Add the roasted bell peppers, tomato paste, olive oil, pomegranate molasses, vinegar, cumin, red pepper flakes, onion powder, allspice, and salt and pepper to taste. Add the reserved pasta water and process until smooth and well mixed. Add the sauce to the pasta and broccoli and toss to combine and heat through. Serve hot.

MAKES 4 SERVINGS

Kitchen-Sink Capellini

As the name implies, there's everything but the kitchen sink in this delicious pasta dish, including artichoke hearts, Kalamata olives, and two kinds of tomatoes. Made with quick-cooking capellini, this meal is ready in just minutes with a complex flavor that belies its speedy preparation.

8 ounces capellini or angel hair pasta
Salt
2 tablespoons olive oil
3 garlic cloves, finely minced
2 (14-ounce) cans fire-roasted diced tomatoes, undrained
1 (16-ounce) can cannellini beans, drained and rinsed
1/3 cup oil-packed or reconstituted sun-dried tomatoes, cut into thin strips
1 (6-ounce) jar marinated artichoke hearts, drained and chopped
1/2 cup Kalamata olives, pitted and halved
4 cups baby spinach or 1 cup chopped frozen spinach, thawed and squeezed (optional)
2 tablespoons fresh chopped basil or 1 teaspoon dried
Ground black pepper
1/4 cup toasted pine nuts or chopped walnuts

Cook the pasta in a pot of boiling salted water until just tender, about 4 minutes. Drain the pasta in a colander. Drizzle with 1 tablespoon of the olive oil, toss to coat, and set aside.

In the same pot in which you cooked the pasta, heat the remaining 1 tablespoon of the oil over medium heat. Add the garlic and cook until fragrant, 30 seconds. Stir in the diced tomatoes, cannellini beans, artichoke hearts, olives, spinach (if using), basil, and salt and pepper to taste. Cook over medium heat until hot and well combined, about 5 minutes. Add the reserved pasta and toss gentle to combine and heat through. Serve hot sprinkled with the pine nuts.

MAKES 4 SERVINGS

Artichoke-Cannelini Linguine

White beans and artichokes are sautéed with onion, capers, and lemon juice to make a sparkling picatta-inspired sauce for pasta.

> 8 ounces linguine or other pasta
> Salt
> 2 tablespoons olive oil
> 1 (14-ounce) can artichoke hearts, drained, quartered, and blotted dry
> Salt and ground black pepper
> 2 tablespoons vegan butter
> 1/4 cup minced yellow onion
> 3 garlic cloves, minced
> 3 tablespoons dry white wine
> 1 (15-ounce) can cannellini beans
> 2 tablespoons capers
> 1/2 teaspoon red pepper flakes, optional
> 3 tablespoons lemon juice
> 2 tablespoons fresh chopped parsley, optional

Cook the pasta in a pot of boiling salted water until it is just tender.

While the pasta is cooking, heat the oil in a skillet over medium-high heat. Add the artichokes and cook until nicely browned all over. Remove from the skillet. Season lightly with salt and pepper and set aside. Put the skillet back on the stove over medium heat. Add the vegan butter and allow to melt. When the butter is melted, add the onion and garlic and cook for 4 minutes or until the onion softens. Add the wine, beans, capers, and red pepper flakes, if using. Continue to cook for 2 to 3 minutes, stirring to heat through. Return the artichokes to the skillet and heat through. Taste and adjust the seasonings, if needed.

When the pasta is done cooking, drain it and transfer it to a large serving bowl or divide it among individual shallow bowls or plates. Top with the artichoke and bean mixture. Serve hot, sprinkled with parsley, if using.

MAKES 4 SERVINGS

Penne with White Beans and Olivada

Olivada is a rich Mediterranean olive paste that goes great with pasta. I like to make it myself so I can add as much garlic and other ingredients to my own taste but you can instead buy it ready-made or substitute a jar of black olive tapenade. Be advised: This recipe is for card-carrying olive-lovers.

8 ounces penne or other bite-size pasta
Salt
1 1/2 cups brine-cured black olives, pitted
2 garlic cloves, smashed
1 tablespoon chopped capers
1 teaspoon dried basil
1/2 teaspoon red pepper flakes
1 1/2 tablespoons balsamic vinegar
3 tablespoons olive oil
1 (15.5-ounce) can Great Northern or other white beans, drained
2 tablespoons chopped fresh parsley, optional

Cook the pasta in a pot of boiling salted water until it is al dente. Reserve 1/2 cup of the hot cooking water.

While the pasta is cooking, pulse the olives and garlic in a food processor until finely chopped. Add the capers, basil, red pepper flakes, vinegar, oil, and process to a paste. Add the reserved pasta water and process to incorporate. Set aside.

When the pasta is done cooking, place the beans in a colander and drain the pasta into the colander. This will heat and rinse the beans at the same time. Place the drained pasta and beans in a large serving bowl or return to the pot. Add the reserved olivada and toss gently to combine. Serve hot, sprinkled with parsley, if using.

MAKES 4 SERVINGS

Rotini with Creamy Pumpkin Sauce and Walnuts

Pasta tossed with a creamy sage-infused sauce sprinkled with walnuts is good enough to make you forget this is pantry cuisine.

    8 ounces rotini or other bite-sized pasta
    Salt
    1 tablespoon olive oil
    1 small onion, minced
    3 cloves garlic, minced
    1 teaspoon ground sage
    1/4 teaspoon red pepper flakes
    1/4 cup dry white wine
    1 (15-ounce) can solid-pack pumpkin
    1 1/2 cups vegetable broth
    1 teaspoon salt, plus more to taste
    1/4 teaspoon ground black pepper
    1 cup plain unsweetened almond milk
    1/2 cup chopped toasted walnuts
    1/4 cup chopped fresh parsley

Cook the pasta in a pot of boiling salted water until just tender.

While the pasta cooks, heat the oil in a saucepan over medium heat. Add the onion, cover and cook for 4 minutes. Stir in the garlic, sage, and red pepper flakes and cook for 30 seconds, then stir in the wine, pumpkin, broth, salt, and pepper. Cook over medium heat, stirring, until smooth and hot, then stir in the almond milk. Taste and adjust the seasonings, if needed.

When the pasta is done cooking, drain it and return it to the pot. Add the reserved sauce and toss to combine. Serve hot sprinkled with the toasted walnuts and parsley.

MAKES 4 SERVINGS

Pasta Marinara

I always keep a jar or two of prepared marinara sauce in the pantry, but when I have time, I prefer to make it myself using good quality canned tomato products. (I only use fresh tomatoes in sauce when they are in peak season in the summer.) This is a good basic sauce that benefits from additions such as sautéed sliced mushrooms, roasted diced eggplant, vegan burger crumbles, or cooked vegan meatballs.

Tip: If you put the pasta water on to boil at the same time you start cooking the sauce, the pasta and sauce will be ready at the same time.

1 tablespoon olive oil
4 garlic cloves, minced
1 tablespoon dehydrated minced onion
2 teaspoons dried basil
1 teaspoon dried oregano
1/4 teaspoon red pepper flakes
1/4 cup dry red wine
1 (28-ounce) can crushed tomatoes
Pinch of sugar
Salt and ground black pepper
8 ounces of your favorite pasta

Heat the oil in a saucepan over medium heat. Add the garlic and cook until fragrant, 30 seconds. Add the onion, basil, oregano, and red pepper flakes. Stir in the red wine and simmer for 1 minute. Add the tomatoes, sugar, and salt and pepper to taste. Simmer over low heat while you cook the pasta.

Cook the pasta in a large pot of boiling salted water until just tender. Drain well. Serve the pasta topped with the sauce. Serve hot.

MAKES 4 SERVINGS

Manchurian Black Bean Noodles

One taste of this easy and elegant dish will convince you that black is the new pasta. Look for black bean pasta in natural food stores or online – it's even available at Costco as of this writing. Low in carbs, high in protein, with a sturdy texture and hearty flavor, black bean pasta is best with an assertive sauce and nothing says assertive like Manchurian sauce. Here, I combine the sauce with black beans for even more protein. Serve with a green salad or make it a one-dish meal and top it with roasted cauliflower florets or other cooked veggie of choice. Of course, if you don't have black bean linguine, you can substitute any noodles you may have on hand.

- 1 (8-ounce) package black bean linguine (or other pasta)
- 1 tablespoon safflower oil
- 5 cloves garlic, minced
- 1 tablespoon grated ginger
- 2 1/2 tablespoons soy sauce
- 1 tablespoon sambal oelek or other Asian chili paste
- 1 1/2 tablespoons ketchup
- 2 teaspoons rice vinegar
- 2 teaspoons sugar
- 1/2 teaspoon onion powder
- 1/4 teaspoon cayenne
- 1 (15-ounce) can black beans, rinsed and drained
- 1/2 cup water
- 2 tablespoons chopped scallion, optional
- 2 tablespoons chopped cilantro, optional

Cook the pasta according to package directions.

While the pasta is cooking, heat the oil in a skillet over medium heat. Add the garlic and ginger, and cook until fragrant, 30 seconds. Stir in the soy sauce, sambal oelek, ketchup, vinegar, sugar, onion powder, and cayenne. Add the black beans and water and bring just to a boil, stirring to mix well. Partially mash the beans while stirring to make a thicker sauce.

When the pasta is cooked, drain it and transfer to a large serving bowl or individual shallow bowls. Top with the sauce and garnish with scallions and cilantro, if using. Serve hot.

MAKES 3 TO 4 SERVINGS

Speedy Lasagna

Even with its 30-minute baking time, this lasagna assembles quickly and can be on your table in well under an hour. When you soften the lasagna noodles in boiling water, you eliminate the need to precook them (and no pot to wash). Using a jarred marinara sauce makes for a quicker assembly, but you can use the sauce on page 126, if you prefer.

9 lasagna noodles
1 (15.5-ounce) can white beans, drained
14 ounces firm tofu, drained
1/3 cup nutritional yeast
1 teaspoon dried basil
1 teaspoon dried parsley
1/2 teaspoon dried oregano
1/2 teaspoon onion powder
1/2 teaspoon garlic powder
Salt and ground black pepper
1 (28-ounce) jar marinara sauce

Arrange the lasagna noodles in a large shallow baking dish and cover with boiling water. Set aside to soften while you make the filling.

In a bowl, combine the white beans, tofu, nutritional yeast, basil parsley, oregano, onion powder, garlic powder, and salt and pepper to taste. Use a potato masher with small holes to mash the mixture until smooth and well combined. Taste and adjust the seasonings, if needed.

Remove the softened noodles from the baking dish and pour off the water. Spread a thin layer of marinara sauce in the bottom of the baking dish and place 3 of the softened noodles on top. Spread half of the tofu and bean mixture on top of the noodles, and top with 3 more noodles. Spread a small amount of sauce on top and spread the remaining filling mixture over it.

Top with the remaining 3 noodles and spread the remaining sauce over the noodles. Cover tightly and bake for 30 minutes or until the filling is hot. Remove from oven and let stand for 5 minutes before serving.

MAKES 4 TO 6 SERVINGS

Noodles with Spicy Peanut Sauce

The operative words here are "noodles" and "peanut sauce" – other additions only add the the deliciousness, so plan to make this when you have veggies you want yo use up or leftover veggies. Bulk up the protein by adding some seitan, tempeh, tofu, or reconstituted Soy Curls. If you don't have thin rice noodles (that require soaking rather than cooking in boiling water), you can use ramen noodles instead or use leftover cooked spaghetti or linguine.

8 ounces very thin rice noodles
1/2 cup peanut butter
3 tablespoons tamari or other soy sauce
2 teaspoons lime or lemon juice
1 teaspoon brown sugar
1/2 teaspoon red pepper flakes, or to taste
1 cup water
2 cups cooked vegetables or other add-ins (see headnote)
2 tablespoons chopped roasted peanuts

Soak the noodles in boiling water until soft, about 15 minutes. While the noodles are softening, prepare the sauce.

In a bowl, whisk together the peanut butter, tamari, lime juice, sugar, red pepper flakes, and 1/2 cup of the water. Blend until smooth.

Transfer the peanut sauce to a large pot and stir in as much of the remaining water as needed to give it a desirable consistency. Heat the sauce over low heat, stirring until it is hot. Drain the softened noodles and add to the pot.

Stir in the cooked vegetables (or other add-ins) and heat through until hot, tossing gently to combine. Serve sprinkled with the peanuts.

MAKES 4 SERVINGS

Spaghetti Lo-Mein

If you are using leftover cooked pasta, steam the broccoli for 3 to 5 minutes. If you don't have fresh vegetables on hand for this recipe, substitute frozen stir-fry vegetables, cooked according to package directions.

8 ounces spaghetti
Salt
2 cups small broccoli florets
2 tablespoons tamari or other soy sauce
3 tablespoons cup hoisin sauce
1 teaspoon toasted sesame oil
1 teaspoon sriracha (optional)
1/4 cup water
2 tablespoons dry sherry (optional)
1 tablespoon safflower oil
3 cloves garlic, minced
1 red bell pepper, cut into strips
2 cups sliced mushrooms
1 carrot, shredded
1/3 cup sliced scallions
2 teaspoons grated fresh ginger
1 cup reconstituted Soy Curls (optional)

Cook the spaghetti in a large pot of boiling salted water until just tender. About 3 to 5 minutes before the pasta is done cooking, add the broccoli. Drain the pasta and broccoli and set aside.

While the pasta is cooking, combine the tamari, hoisin, sesame oil, and sriracha, if using. Add the water and sherry, if using. Mix well and set aside.

Heat the safflower oil in a large skillet or wok over medium-high heat. Add the garlic, bell pepper, mushrooms, carrot, scallions, and ginger. Cook, stirring frequently, until tender, about 3 minutes. Add the Soy Curls, if using and stir to combine. Stir in the reserved noodles and the sauce mixture, and gently toss to combine until heated through. Taste and adjust the seasonings, if needed. Serve hot.

MAKES 4 SERVINGS

7

Sweet Treats

Easy as Chocolate Pie

This decadent chocolate pie assembles in minutes. After some time in the fridge, it's ready to serve. What can be easier than that?

12 ounces vegan semisweet chocolate chips
1/4 cup almond milk or other nondairy milk
1 tablespoon coconut oil
1/2 cup chopped nuts (optional)
1/2 cup sweetened dried cranberries, cherries, or blueberries (optional)
1 vegan chocolate cookie crust (Keebler's brand is vegan-friendly)
Chocolate curls or chopped nuts, for garnish

In a saucepan, combine the chocolate chips, almond milk, and coconut oil over medium heat. Cook, stirring until the chocolate and coconut oil are melted. Stir in the nuts and dried fruit, if using, until well combined.

Transfer the chocolate mixture to the crust and spread evenly. Refrigerate for at least 3 hours to firm up before serving. Garnish the top with chocolate curls.

MAKES 8 SERVINGS

Peanutty Energy Balls

Like a bite-sized granola bar, these tasty bites make terrific energy-boosting between-meal snacks. They also make a fun, hassle-free breakfast.

- 1/4 cup peanut butter
- 2 tablespoons maple syrup
- 2 tablespoons apple juice (or other fruit juice)
- 1 1/2 cups vegan granola
- 1/2 cup ground peanuts or other nuts (optional)

In a food processor, combine the peanut butter, maple syrup, and juice and process until smooth and well blended.

Add the granola and pulse to mix well. Use your hands to pinch off a small amount of the mixture and roll it into a 1-inch ball. Repeat until all of the mixture is used. Roll the balls in ground peanuts, if desired, and arrange them on a plate.

MAKES ABOUT 12

Almond-Cranberry Haystacks

Here's an updated version of an old family favorite. For variety, use vegan white chocolate or butterscotch chips and change up the type of nut or dried fruit. For a "salted chocolate" version, sprinkle the tops with a few grains of coarse sea salt.

- 12 ounces semisweet vegan chocolate chips
- 1/2 cup dried cranberries
- 1/2 cup toasted slivered almonds
- 1 1/2 cups chow mein noodles

Melt the chocolate in a metal bowl over a saucepan of boiling water. When the chocolate is melted, stir in the almonds, noodles, and cranberries. Mix well.

Use a teaspoon to drop the warm mixture into small mounds onto a baking sheet lined with parchment paper or waxed paper. Refrigerate to firm up.

MAKES ABOUT 24

Chocolate-Coated Walnut-Stuffed Dates in Pastry

This is actually two recipes in one. The quick version takes just minutes (plus chilling time) for chewy-crunchy chocolate-covered walnut-stuffed dates. For added decadence, take the extra step of wrapping the stuffed dates in pastry and baking them.

12 walnut halves
12 pitted dates
3/4 cup vegan chocolate chips
1 sheet vegan puff pastry, thawed

Stuff a walnut half into each of the dates and set aside. Melt the chocolate in a heatproof bowl in the microwave or on the stovetop in a double boiler. Place the stuffed dates into the melted chocolate, turning to coat. Remove each coated date from the chocolate and arrange on a plate or baking sheet lined with parchment paper or waxed paper. Refrigerate for several hours to firm up. You can serve these now for a quick version (minus the pastry). Or proceed with the next step.

Cut the puff pastry into 12 (3-inch) squares. Place a chilled date on top of each piece of pastry and bring up the sides. Pinch the seams to seal and then roll in your hands to form a smooth ball. Arrange the pastry-wrapped dates on a baking sheet and refrigerate for an hour or longer to chill.

When ready to bake, preheat the oven to 400°F. Bake until nicely browned all over, 15 to 20 minutes. Cool for 10 minutes before serving.

MAKES 12

Coconut Lime Drops

These luscious bites deliver a refreshing taste of the tropics. They soften a bit at room temperature, so store any leftovers in the refrigerator. I have it on good authority that these taste great served with vegan strawberry ice cream.

- 1 cup almond flour
- 3/4 cup coconut flour
- 1/4 cup agave nectar or maple syrup
- 1/3 cup lime juice
- 1 tablespoon water
- 2 teaspoons vanilla extract
- 1/4 cup coconut oil, melted
- Shredded coconut, for rolling (optional)

In a food processor, combine all the ingredients and process until it forms a smooth dough.

Scoop out a teaspoonful of the mixture and roll it in the palms of your hand into a 1-inch ball. Repeat with the remaining mixture until it is all used. Roll the balls in shredded coconut, if using. Arrange the balls on a baking sheet lined with parchment paper and refrigerate until firm, 15 minutes. Keep refrigerated until ready to serve.

MAKES ABOUT 24

No-Bake Oatmeal Cookies

These easy cookies are filled with goodness and can be changed up to suit your mood. For example: substitute dried cranberries or raisins for a portion of the dates; use different nuts or substitute chocolate chips for all or part of the nuts; eliminate the cinnamon; use agave instead of maple syrup.

2 cups soft Medjool dates, pitted
1 cup walnut or pecan pieces
1 cup old-fashioned rolled oats
1/4 cup maple syrup
2 tablespoons coconut oil or vegan butter, melted
1 teaspoon vanilla extract
3/4 teaspoon ground cinnamon
1/4 teaspoon salt

In a food processor, combine the dates, nuts, and oats, and process until crumbly. Add the maple syrup, coconut oil, vanilla, cinnamon, and salt and process until it holds together in a mass. If the mixture is too dry to hold together add a little water, 1 tablespoon at a time.

Scoop out about 1 tablespoon of the dough and roll it between your hands to form a ball. Repeat until all the dough is used, arranging them on a baking sheet lined with parchment paper. Use a fork to press down on the cookies to flatten them slightly and make a criss-cross pattern. Refrigerate for 3 to 4 hours to firm up before serving. Keep leftovers covered and refrigerated.

MAKES ABOUT 24

Rawklava

These tasty bites are a great way to enjoy the flavor of baklava without the pastry.

- 2 cups walnut pieces
- 1/2 cup pistachios
- 1/4 cup coconut flour
- 2/3 cup pitted dates
- 1/2 cup soft golden raisins
- 3 tablespoons agave nectar

In a food processor, combine the walnuts, pistachios, and flour, and pulse until the nuts are evenly ground (do not overprocess). Add the dates, raisins, and 1 tablespoon of the agave, and pulse until the mixture is well incorporated and moist. (Add a little water, 2 teaspoons at a time, if needed.)

Press the mixture firmly and evenly into an 8-inch square baking pan lined with plastic wrap or roll out on flat surface between two sheets of parchment paper, then transfer to a baking sheet and remove the top paper, pressing the mixture on the sides to make an 8-inch square.

Use a pastry brush to spread the remaining agave evenly across the top. Refrigerate for at least 3 hours, then remove from the pan and transfer to a cutting board. Cut the rawklava into 1 1/2-inch squares and arrange on a plate to serve. Store leftovers in an airtight container in the refrigerator.

MAKES ABOUT 2 DOZEN

Bananas Foster Dessert Nachos

Lightly sweetened tortilla chips add a crunchy new spin on Bananas Foster, a favorite dessert in our house.

Nacho chips
3 tablespoons melted vegan butter
2 tablespoons finely ground light brown sugar
1/4 teaspoon ground cinnamon
2 to 3 (10-inch) flour tortillas

Bananas
2 tablespoons vegan butter
1/2 cup pecan halves or pieces
1/4 cup natural or light brown sugar
4 ripe bananas, sliced
3 tablespoons dark rum

To serve
4 scoops vegan vanilla ice cream

Nacho chips: Preheat oven to 350 degrees F. Place a tortilla on a work surface and brush one side of the tortilla with the melted butter. Combine the sugar and cinnamon in a small bowl and mix to combine. Sprinkle the tortilla with cinnamon sugar and cut it into wedges. Arrange the tortilla wedges on a large baking sheet in a single layer. Repeat with the remaining tortillas. (You may need to do this in batches) Bake for about 8 minutes. Remove from the oven and set aside to cools for about 10 minutes.

Bananas: While the chips are cooling, heat the butter in a medium skillet over medium heat. Add the pecan pieces and the sugar, and cook, stirring for 3 minutes to dissolve the sugar. Add the rum and cook for 1 minute longer, then add the banana slices, stirring gently to coat. Cook 1 minute longer to warm the bananas.

To serve: Divide the chips among 4 shallow bowls. Top each with a scoop of ice cream, then top each with a portion of the banana mixture, dividing evenly. Serve immediately.

MAKES 4 SERVINGS

Stovetop Peach-Blueberry Crumble

Similar to a fruit crisp, this dessert is made in a skillet on a stovetop instead of in the oven. The basis of the "crumble" topping is healthful, toothsome oatmeal. Yum.

- 1 1/2 pounds firm, ripe peaches (5 to 6 peaches)
- 1 tablespoon lemon juice
- 1/2 cup granulated sugar
- 2 tablespoons cornstarch
- 1 cup fresh or frozen blueberries
- 1 cup old-fashioned or quick-cooking oats
- 1/2 cup light brown sugar
- 1/4 teaspoon salt
- 1/2 teaspoon ground cinnamon
- 1/2 cup cold vegan butter (Earth Balance), diced

Halve and cut the peaches, then cut them into thin slices and place in a large bowl. Add the lemon juice, sugar, and cornstarch and toss well to combine. Gently fold in the blueberries. Transfer the fruit mixture to a 10-inch skillet (cast iron is preferable) and set aside.

In a food processor, combine the oats, brown sugar, cinnamon, and salt and pulse to combine and break down the oats somewhat. Add the butter and pulse until the pieces of butter are the size of peas.

Sprinkle the topping mixture evenly over the fruit. Cover and cook over medium heat until hot and bubbly, about 15 minutes. Turn off heat, remove the lid, and let stand for another 5 minutes to cool slightly. Serve warm or at room temperature.

MAKES 4 TO 6 SERVINGS

Chocolate-Almond Truffles

Just four ingredients comprise these little beauties that are best eaten after they have time to firm up in the fridge.

> 1/2 cup vegan semi-sweet chocolate chips
> 1/2 cup confectioners' sugar
> 1/4 cup almond butter
> 1/3 cup finely crushed toasted slivered

Melt the chocolate in a metal bowl over a saucepan of simmering with boiling water.

Remove from heat and stir in the sugar and almond butter, mixing until well combined.

Use your hands to shape the mixture into 1-inch balls and set on a plate lined with plastic film wrap.

Roll the balls in the crushed almonds and refrigerate for at least 1 hour to firm up a bit.

MAKES 10 TO 12

No-Fuss Chocolate Fondue

Fondue is easy to assemble, fun to eat, and delicious in the bargain. What better way to while away the hours than by dipping chunks of cake, cookies, fruit, and pretzels into a pot of warm rich chocolate laced with your favorite liqueur?

    8 ounces vegan semisweet chocolate
    1/2 cup almond milk or other nondairy milk
    3 tablespoons sugar
    1 to 2 tablespoons liqueur of choice (optional; we like Frangelico)
    Assorted fresh, canned, or reconstituted dried fruit for dipping, cut into bite-size pieces
        as necessary (pears, pineapple, etc.)
    Vegan cake or cookies, cut into bite-sized pieces
    Pretzel sticks, etc.

Finely chop the chocolate into pieces and place in a fondue pot. Light the tea candle or sterno under the fondue pot, cover, and stir the chocolate occasionally until melted.

Blend in the almond milk and sugar. Stir in the liqueur, if using. Cover and let the mixture continue to heat until the chocolate mixture is hot. (Note: If you don't have a fondue pot, melt the chocolate mixture in a metal bowl over a saucepan of simmering water. You can leave it in the bowl to serve.)

Arrange the "dippers" on plates and set them on the table with fondue forks or wooden skewers. Let everyone dig in.

MAKES 4 SERVINGS

Ginger-Walnut Rum Balls

The best thing about this recipe, in addition to getting to drink the leftover rum, is that no baking or refrigeration is needed to make them. In fact, they benefit from sitting out at room temperature. If you're not a fan of ginger snaps, substitute vanilla wafers. For a non-alcoholic version, use apple juice in place of the rum.

- 1 cup finely crushed vegan gingersnap crumbs
- 1/2 cup plus 1/4 cup confectioners' sugar
- 1/4 cup finely crushed walnuts
- 2 tablespoons dark rum
- 2 tablespoons maple syrup

In a bowl, combine cookie crumbs, 1/2 cup of the confectioners' sugar, the ground nuts, rum, and maple syrup. Use your hands to mix together thoroughly until the mixture holds together.

Use your hands to shape the mixture into 1-inch balls. Roll the balls in remaining 1/4 cup confectioners' sugar and arrange on a plate. Cover with plastic film wrap and let sit for several hours or overnight to allow flavors to develop.

MAKES 18

Mangos with Pistachios and Cranberries

If fresh ripe mangoes are unavailable, use thawed frozen mango chunks. Sprinkle with pistachios and dried cranberries, and finish with a sprig of mint, for an easy and delicious dessert. This is best served at room temperature to bring out the flavor of the fruit.

- 2 fresh ripe mangoes, peeled, pitted and diced or 2 cups frozen mango chunks, thawed
- 1/4 cup chopped pistachio nuts
- 2 tablespoons sweetened dried cranberries
- Mint leaves, for garnish

Divide the diced mango among four dessert glasses or bowls. Sprinkle with pistachios and cranberries. Garnish with mint leaves and serve.

MAKES 4 SERVINGS

Fudgy Brownie Mug

This single-serve brownie mug is ideal for satisfying that chocolate craving quickly and without having to bake an entire pan of brownies.

1/4 cup all-purpose flour
2 tablespoons unsweetened cocoa
1/4 teaspoon baking powder
2 tablespoons maple syrup or agave nectar
2 tablespoons applesauce
2 tablespoons nondairy milk
2 tablespoons semisweet vegan chocolate chips

In a large mug, combine the flour, cocoa, and baking powder. Mix well, then stir in the maple syrup, applesauce, and nondairy milk. Mix well, stirring until well combined. Stir in the chocolate chips. Microwave on High for 2 minutes, or a bit longer, depending on your microwave. The center of the brownie should still be slightly moist. Set aside to cool for a few minutes.

MAKES 1 SERVING

Pecan Pie Balls

These chewy-crunchy balls of goodness taste very much like pecan pie with none of the fuss or baking time.

- 1 cup pitted dates
- 1 cup pecan pieces
- 1/2 cup flaked coconut
- 1 tablespoon almond butter or other nut butter
- 1 tablespoon agave nectar
- 1/2 teaspoon vanilla extract

Soak the dates in a bowl of warm water for 15 minutes, then drain well and transfer to a food processor.

Add the pecans, coconut, almond butter, agave, and vanilla. Pulse until well combined, leaving some texture.

Use your hands to shape the mixture into 1-inch balls and arrange on a platter. Serve as is or cover and refrigerate until chilled to firm a little before serving.

MAKES ABOUT 16

Acknowledgments

I want to thank my husband Jon for two reasons. First, for being my co-author of *Vegan Unplugged,* the previous incarnation of this book that featured his humor, anecdotes, and survival tips for when the power goes out. Second, for believing in my pantry recipes enough to publish this totally new version that now includes fresh ingredients and lots of new recipes.

Many thanks to Annie Oliverio for her gorgeous photos and for making these simple inexpensive pantry meals look like a million bucks.

I also want to thank Lyndsay Orwig for testing the new recipes in this book, as well as Debbie Blicher for her editing and proofreading skills.

Most of all, I want to thank the readers of *Vegan Unplugged* for their kind words about that book and their enthusiastic requests for a fresh new take on the recipes. Thank you all for reminding me that quick-and-easy recipes are appreciated come rain or shine.

About the Author

Robin Robertson has worked with food for over 30 years as a restaurant chef, caterer, cooking teacher, and food writer. She is the author of more than twenty cookbooks including the best-sellers *Vegan Planet, One-Dish Vegan, Quick-Fix Vegan,* and *Vegan Without Borders.*

Robin has been a regular columnist for both *VegNews Magazine* and *Vegetarian Times* and has written articles for *Cooking Light, Health, Better Nutrition, Health Naturally,* and *Restaurant Business Magazine.* Robin is active on social media as well as her website, www.RobinRobertson.com.

Index

Metric Conversions and Equivalents

The recipes in this book have not been tested with metric measurements, so some variations may occur.

LIQUID	
U.S.	METRIC
1 tsp	5 ml
1 tbs	15 ml
2 tbs	30 ml
1/4 cup	60 ml
1/3 cup	75 ml
1/2 cup	120 ml
2/3 cup	150 ml
3/4 cup	180 ml
1 cup	240 ml
1 1/4 cups	300 ml
1 1/3 cups	325 ml
1 1/2 cups	350 ml
1 2/3 cups	375 ml
1 3/4 cups	400 ml
2 cups (1 pint)	475 ml
3 cups	720 ml
4 cups (1 quart)	945 ml

GENERAL METRIC CONVERSION FORMULAS	
Ounces to grams	ounces x 28.35 = grams
Grams to ounces	grams x 0.035 = ounces
Pounds to grams	pounds x 435.5 = grams
Pounds to kilograms	pounds x 0.45 = kilograms
Cups to liters	cups x 0.24 = liters
Fahrenheit to Celsius	(°F - 32) x 5 ÷ 9 = °C
Celsius to Fahrenheit	(°C x 9) ÷ 5 + 32 = °F

WEIGHT	
U.S.	METRIC
1/2 oz	14 g
1 oz	28 g
1 1/2 oz	43 g
2 oz	57 g
21/2 oz	71 g
4 oz	113 g
5 oz	142 g
6 oz	170 g
7 oz	200 g
8 oz (1/2 lb)	227 g
9 oz	255 g
10 oz	284 g
11 oz	312 g
12 oz	340 g
13 oz	368 g
14 oz	400 g
15 oz	425 g
16 oz (1 lb)	454 g

OVEN TEMPERATURE		
°F	Gas Mark	°C
250	1/2	120
275	1	140
300	2	150
325	3	165
350	4	180
375	5	190
400	6	200
425	7	220
450	8	230
475	9	240
500	10	260
550	Broil	290

LENGTH	
U.S.	Metric
1/2 inch	1.25 cm
1 inch	2.5 cm
6 inches	15 cm
8 inches	20 cm
10 inches	25 cm
12 inches	30 cm